Penguin Modern Poets
VOLUME 12

Helen Dunmore is a poet and novelist. Her poetry collections include
The Sea Skater, winner of the Poetry Society's Alice Hunt Bartlett Award,
The Raw Garden, a Poetry Book Society Choice, and *Secrets*, winner of the
1995 Signal Poetry Award. Her novels are *Zennor in Darkness*, which was
awarded the McKitterick Prize in 1994; *Burning Bright*; *A Spell of Winter*,
winner of the 1996 Orange Prize for Fiction; and *Talking to the Dead*. Her
novels are all published by Penguin.

Jo Shapcott is the first person to win the National Poetry Competition
twice, the second time in 1991 for the widely acclaimed poem 'Phrase
Book'. Her first collection, *Electroplating the Baby*, won a Commonwealth
Prize. Her second book, *Phrase Book*, won a Poetry Book Society Choice.
She is co-editor with Matthew Sweeney of *Emergency Kit: Poems for Strange
Times*, an anthology of contemporary poetry. In 1997 her children's poems
The Creatures Indoors were set for orchestra and narrator by composer
Stephen Montague and premiered by the London Symphony Orchestra.
She was the 1997 Penguin Writers Fellow at the British Library.

Matthew Sweeney was born in 1952 in Donegal, Ireland, and he moved
to London in 1973. Among his books of poetry are *Blue Shoes* (Poetry
Book Society Choice), *Cacti* and *The Bridal Suite*, as well as two collections
for children, *The Flying Spring Onion* and *Fatso in the Red Suit*. With John
Hartley-Williams he has recently published *Writing Poetry*, a practical
book drawing on workshop experience. He does frequent readings and
workshops all over England and elsewhere and he works regularly in
schools. He was Writer in Residence at London's South Bank Centre in
1994–5.

The Penguin Modern Poets Series

Penguin Modern Poets

VOLUME 12

HELEN DUNMORE

JO SHAPCOTT

MATTHEW SWEENEY

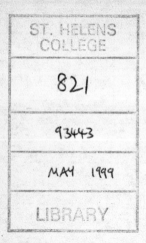
PENGUIN BOOKS

Published by the Penguin Group
Penguin Books Ltd, 27 Wrights Lane, London w8 5tz, England
Penguin Books USA Inc., 375 Hudson Street, New York, New York 10014, USA
Penguin Books Australia Ltd, Ringwood, Victoria, Australia
Penguin Books Canada Ltd, 10 Alcorn Avenue, Toronto, Ontario, Canada m4v 3b2
Penguin Books (NZ) Ltd, 182–190 Wairau Road, Auckland 10, New Zealand

Penguin Books Ltd, Registered Offices: Harmondsworth, Middlesex, England

This selection first published 1997
10 9 8 7 6 5 4 3 2 1

Set in 10.5/13pt Monotype Garamond
Typeset by Rowland Phototypesetting Ltd, Bury St Edmunds, Suffolk
Printed in England by Clays Ltd, St Ives plc

Contents

Helen Dunmore

Candle poem

(after Sa'di Yusuf)

A candle for the ship's breakfast
eaten while moving southward
through mild grey water
with the work all done,
a candle for the house seen from outside,
the voices and shadows
of the moment before coming home,

a candle for the noise of aeroplanes
going elsewhere, passing over,
for delayed departures, embarrassed silences
between people who love one another,
a candle for sandwiches in service stations
at four am, and the taste of coffee
from plastic cups, thickened with sugar
to keep us going,

a candle for the crowd around a coffin
and the terrible depth it has to fall
into the grave dug for everyone,
the deaths for decades to come,
our deaths; a candle for going home
and feeling hungry after saying
we would never be able to eat the ham,
the fruit cake, those carefully-buttered buns.

At the Emporium

He is the one you can count on
for yesterday's bread, rolling tobacco
and the staccato
tick of the blinds
on leathery Wednesday afternoons.
He has hand-chalked boards with the prices
of Anchor butter and British wine.
He doesn't hold with half-day closing.

He's the king of long afternoons
lounging vested in his doorway.
He watches the children dwindle
and dawdle, licking icepops
that drip on the steps.
His would be the last face that saw them
before an abduction. Come in,
he is always open.

He lived next door all his life

One year he painted his front door yellow.
It was the splash of a carrier bag
in the dun terrace,
but for the rest he was inconspicuous.

He went out one way and came back the other,
often carrying laundry and once compost
for the tree he thought might do in the back yard.
Some time later there was its skeleton
taking up most of the bin.

He passed the remark 'It's a pity'
when it rained on a Saturday,
and of a neighbour's child he said 'terror'.
He picked his words like scones from a plate,

dropping no crumbs. When his front door shut
he was more gone than last Christmas.
But for the girls stored in his cellar
to learn what it meant
to have no pity, to be terror,
he was there.

The surgeon husband

Here at my worktop, foil-wrapping a silver salmon
– yes, a whole salmon – I'm thinking
of the many bodies of women
that my husband daily opens.

Here he lunges at me in Wellingtons.
He is up to his armpits, a fisherman
tugging against the strength of the current.

I imagine the light for him, clean,
and a green robing of willow
and the fish hammering upstream.

I too tug at the flaps of the salmon
where its belly was, trying to straighten
the silver seams before they are sewn.
We are one in our dreams.

The epidural is patchy, his assistant's
handwriting is slipping. At eleven fifteen
they barb their patient to sleep, jot 'knife to skin',
and the nurse smiles over her mask at the surgeon.

But I am quietly dusting out the fish-kettle,
and I have the salmon clean as a baby
grinning at me from the table.

Fishing beyond sunset

The boy in the boat, the tip of the pole,
slow swing of the boat as the wash goes round
from other boats with lights on, heading home
to islands, from islands: anyway they come.

Thirty-four bass, small bass, not worth keeping.
See them in the water, the hang
of twice-caught fish playing dumb,
then the shake-off of air. The kickdown

always surprises you, makes your feet grip
on the planks of the boat. There is the line
disappearing into the sunset
or so it seems, but it is plumbed

by your finger, which sees nothing
but a breeze of line running through water.
Behind you a sheet of fire
does something to pole, to boat, to boy.

We are men, not beasts

We are men, not beasts,
though we fall in the dark
on the rattlesnake's path
and flinch with fire of fear
running over our flesh
and beat it to death,

we are men, not beasts
and we walk upright
with the moss-feathered dark
like a shawl on our shoulders
and we carry fire
steeply, inside a cage of fingers,

we are men, not beasts,
and what we cannot help wanting
we banish – the barn yawn, the cow breath,
the stickiness we come from.

All the things you are not yet

for Tess

Tonight there's a crowd in my head:
all the things you are not yet.
You are words without paper, pages
sighing in summer forests, gardens
where builders stub out their rubble
and plastic oozes its sweat.
All the things you are, you are not yet.

Not yet the lonely window in midwinter
with the whine of tea on an empty stomach,
not yet the heating you can't afford and must wait for,
tamping a coin in on each hour.
Not the gorgeous shush of restaurant doors
and their interiors, always so much smaller.
Not the smell of the newsprint, the blur
on your fingertips – your fame. Not yet

the love you will have for Winter Pearmains
and Chanel No 5 – and then your being unable
to buy both washing-machine and computer
when your baby's due to be born,
and my voice saying, 'I'll get you one'
and you frowning, frowning
at walls and surfaces which are not mine –
all this, not yet. Give me your hand,

that small one without a mark of work on it,
the one that's strange to the washing-up bowl
and doesn't know Fairy Liquid from whiskey.
Not yet the moment of your arrival in taxis
at daring destinations, or your being alone at stations
with the skirts of your fashionable clothes flapping
and no money for the telephone.

Not yet the moment when I can give you nothing
so well-folded it fits in an envelope –
a dull letter you won't reread.
Not yet the moment of your assimilation
in that river flowing westward: river of clothes,
of dreams, an accent unlike my own
saying to someone I don't know: *darling* . . .

Diving girl

She's next to nowhere, feeling no cold
in her white sluther of bubbles.
She comes to a point like a seal
in his deep dive, she is sleek.
As her nostrils close
she's at home. See how salt water slides
as she opens her eyes.

There is the word *naked*
but she's not spelled by it.
Look at her skin's steel glint
and the knife of her fins.
With the basking shark
with the minke whale
and the grey seal
she comes up to breathe
ten miles offshore.

Russian doll

When I held you up to my cheek you were cold
when I came close to your smile it dissolved,

the paint on your lips was as deep
as the steaming ruby of beetroot soup

but your breath smelled of varnish and pine
and your eyes swivelled away from mine.

When I wanted to open you up
you glowed, dumpy and perfect

smoothing your dozen little selves
like rolls of fat under your apron

and I hadn't the heart to look at them.
I knew I would be spoiling something.

But when I listened to your heart
I heard the worlds inside of you spinning
like the earth on its axis spinning.

That violet-haired lady

That violet-haired lady, dowager-
humped, giving herself so many
smiles, taut glittering smiles,
smiles that swallow the air in front of her,
smiles that cling to shop-mirrors
and mar their silvering, smiles
like a spider's wrinklework
flagged over wasteland bushes –

she's had so many nips and tucks,
so much mouse-delicate
invisible mending. Her youth
squeaks out of its prison –
the dark red bar of her mouth
opening and closing.
She wants her hair to look black,
pure black, so she strands it with violet,
copperleaf, burgundy, rust –
that violet-haired lady, dowager-
humped, giving herself
so many smiles, keeping the light on.

The butcher's daughter

Where have you been, my little daughter
out in the wild weather?

I have met with a sailor, mother,
he has given me five clubs for juggling
and says I must go with him for ever.

Oh no, my treasure
you must come in and stay for ever
for you are the butcher's daughter.

Where have you been, my little daughter
in the winter weather?

I have met a man of war, mother,
he has given me four hoops to dance through
and he says I must love him for ever.

Oh no, my treasure
you must come in and shut the door
for you are the butcher's daughter.

Where have you been, my little daughter,
out in stormy weather?

I have met with a prince, mother,
he has given me three promises
and I must rule his heart for ever.

Oh no, my treasure
you must give back his promises
for you are the butcher's daughter.

Where have you been, my little daughter
in the wild of the weather?

I have spoken to a wise man, mother,
who gave me knowledge of good and evil
and said I must learn from him for ever.

Oh no, my treasure
you have no need of his knowledge
for you are the butcher's daughter.

Where have you been, my little daughter
out in the summer weather?

I have met with a butcher, mother,
and he is sharpening a knife for me
for I am the butcher's daughter.

Breeze of ghosts

Tall ship hanging out at the horizon
tall ship blistering the horizon
you've been there so long
your sheets and decks white
in the sun

what wind whispers you in?

Tall ship creaking at the horizon
your captain long gone
your crew in the cabin
drinking white rum
their breath spiralling

what wind breathes you in?

Tall ship tilting to the shoreline
past Spanish palms
tall ship coming in like a swan
in the midday sun

what wind blows you in?

It is the cool
wind of the morning
stirring my masts
before the sun
burns it to nothing,
they call it
breeze of ghosts.

The greenfield ghost

The greenfield ghost is not much of a ghost,
it is a ghost of dammed-up streams,
it is a ghost of slow walks home
and sunburn and blackberry stains.

The greenfield ghost is not much of a ghost.
It is the ghost of low-grade land,
it is the ghost of lovers holding hands
on evening strolls out of town.

The greenfield ghost is not much of a ghost.
It is the ghost of mothers at dusk calling,
it is the ghost of children leaving their dens
for safe houses which will cover them.

Three ways of recovering a body

By chance I was alone in my bed the morning
I woke to find my body had gone.
It had been coming. I'd cut off my hair in sections
so each of you would have something to remember,
then my nails worked loose from their beds
of oystery flesh. Who was it got them?
One night I slipped out of my skin. It lolloped
hooked to my heels, hurting. I had to spray on
more scent so you could find me in the dark,
I was going so fast. One of you begged for my ears
because you could hear the sea in them.

First I planned to steal myself back. I was a mist
on thighs, belly and hips. I'd slept with so many men.
I was with you in the ash-haunted stations of Poland,
I was with you on that grey plaza in Berlin
while you wolfed three doughnuts without stopping,
thinking yourself alone. Soon I recovered my lips
by waiting behind the mirror while you shaved.
You pouted. I peeled away kisses like wax
no longer warm to the touch. Then I flew off.

Next I decided to become a virgin. Without a body
it was easy to make up a new story. In seven years
every invisible cell would be renewed
and none of them would have touched any of you.
I went to a cold lake, to a grey-lichened island,
I was gold in the wallet of the water.
I was known to the inhabitants, who were in love
with the coveted whisper of my virginity:
all too soon they were bringing me coffee and perfume,
cash under stones. I could really do something for them.

Thirdly I tried marriage to a good husband
who knew my past but forgave it. I believed in the power
of his penis to smoke out all those men
so that bit by bit my body service would resume,
although for a while I'd be the one woman in the world
who was only present in the smile of her vagina.
He stroked the air where I might have been.
I turned to the mirror and saw mist gather
as if someone lived in the glass. Recovering
I breathed to myself, '*Hold on! I'm coming.*'

To Virgil

Lead me with your cold, sure hand,
make me press the correct buttons
on the automatic ticket machine,
make me not present my ticket upside down
to the slit mouth at the barriers,

then make the lift not jam
in the hot dark of the deepest lines.
May I hear the voice on the loudspeaker
and understand each syllable
of the doggerel of stations.

If it is rush-hour, let me be close to the doors,
I do not ask for space,
let no one crush me into a corner
or accidentally squeeze hard on my breasts
or hit me with bags or chew gum in my face.

If there are incidents, let them be over,
let there be no red-and-white tape
marking the place, make it not happen
when the tunnel has wrapped its arms around my train
and the lights have failed.

Float me up the narrow escalator
not looking backward, losing my balance
or letting go of your cold, sure hand.
Let there not be a fire
in the gaps, hold me secure.
Let me come home to the air.

Holiday to lonely

He's going on holiday to lonely
but no one knows. He has got the sunblock
the cash and the baseball cap
shorts that looked nice in the shop
then two days' indoor bicycling
to get his legs ready.

He plans to learn something in lonely.
Bits of the language, new dishes.
He would like to try out a sport –
jet-ski maybe, or fishing.
You are meant to be alone, fishing.
There are books about it at the airport.

In the departure lounge, he has three hours
to learn to harpoon a marlin
and to overhear the history
of that couple quarrelling
about Bourbon and Jamesons –
which is the best way to have fun.

He is starting to like the look of lonely
with its steady climate, its goals
anyone can touch. He settles
for drinking lots of Aqua Libra
and being glad about Airmiles
as the Australian across the aisle
plugs into *Who's That Girl?*

In the desert knowing nothing

Here I am in the desert knowing nothing,
here I am knowing nothing
in the desert of knowing nothing,
here I am in this wide
desert long after midnight

here I am knowing nothing
hearing the noise of the rain
and the melt of fat in the pan

here is our man on the phone knowing something
and here's our man fresh from the briefing
in combat jeans and a clip microphone
testing for sound,
catching the desert rain, knowing something,

here's the general who's good with his men
storming the camera, knowing something
in the pit of his Americanness
here's the general taut in his battledress
and knowing something

here's the boy washing his kit in a tarpaulin
on a front-line he knows from his GCSE
coursework on Wilfred Owen
and knowing something

here is the plane banking,
the *go go go* of adrenalin
the child melting
and here's the grass that grows overnight
from the desert rain, feeling for him
and knowing everything

and here I am knowing nothing
in the desert of knowing nothing
dry from not speaking.

Getting the strap

The Our Father, the moment of fear.
He dodged round us and ran,
but was fetched back again
to stand before us on the platform.

The Our Father, the moment of fear
as the fist gripped and he hung
from the headmaster's arm,
doubling on the spot like a rabbit
blind for home.

The Our Father, the moment of fear.
The watch he'd stolen was given
back to its owner, dumb
in the front row, watching the strapping.

The Our Father, the moment of fear.
The strap was old and black and it cracked
on belly buttock and once across his lip
because he writhed and twisted.
He would not stand and take it.

The Our Father, the moment of fear.
There was a lot of sun
leaking through churchy windows
onto a spurt of urine.
After an age of watching
we sang the last hymn.

The diving reflex

The diving reflex can enable the human body to shut down and maintain
life for as long as forty minutes underwater at low temperatures.

Where the great ship sank I am,
where cathedrals of ice breathe through me
down naves of cold
I tread and roll,

where the light goes
and the pressure weighs
in the rotten caves of an iceberg's side
I glide,

I am mute, not breathing,
my shoulders hunched to the stream
with the whales, drowsing.

Bells rang in my blood
as I went down
purling, heart over heel
through the nonchalant
fish-clad ocean —

her inquisitive kiss
slowed me to this
great cartwheel.

Down I go, tied to my rope.
I have my diving reflex to sister me,
and the blubbery sea cow
nods, knowing me.

There is blood in my veins
too thick for panic,

there is a down
so deep a whale
thins to a sheet of paper
and here I hang.
I will not drown.

Heimat

Deep in busy lizzies and black iron
he sleeps for the Heimat,
and his photograph slips in and out of sight
as if breathing.

There are petals against his cheeks
but he is not handsome.
His small eyes search the graveyard fretfully
and the flesh of his cheeks clouds
the bones of heroism.

No one can stop him being young
and he is so tired of being young.
He would like to feel pain in his joints
as he wanders down to Hübers,
but he's here as always,
always on his way back from the photographer's
in his army collar
with a welt on his neck rubbed raw.

The mountains are white and sly as they always were.
Old women feed the graveyard with flowers,
clear the glass on his photograph
with chamois leathers,
bend and whisper the inscription.
They are his terrible suitors.

The sea skater

A skater comes to this blue pond,
his worn Canadian skates
held by the straps.

He sits on the grass
lacing stiff boots
into a wreath of effort and breath.

He tugs at the straps and they sound
as ice does when weight troubles it
and cracks bloom around stones

creaking in quiet mid-winter
mid-afternoons: a fine time for a skater.
He knows it and gauges the sun
to see how long it will be safe to skate.

Now he hisses and spins in jumps
while powder ice clings to the air
but by trade he's a long-haul skater.

Little villages, stick-like in the cold,
offer a child or a farm-worker
going his round. These watch him
go beating onward between iced alders
seawards, and so they picture him
always smoothly facing forward, foodless and waterless,
mounting the crusted waves on his skates.

Wild strawberries

What I get I bring home to you:
a dark handful, sweet-edged,
dissolving in one mouthful.

I bother to bring them for you
though they're so quickly over,
pulpless, sliding to juice,

a grainy rub on the tongue
and the taste's gone. If you remember
we were in the woods at wild strawberry time

and I was making a basket of dockleaves
to hold what you'd picked,
but the cold leaves unplaited themselves

and slid apart, and again unplaited themselves
until I gave up and ate wild strawberries
out of your hands for sweetness.

I lipped at your palm –
the little salt edge there,
the tang of money you'd handled.

As we stayed in the wood, hidden,
we heard the sound system below us
calling the winners at Chepstow,
faint as the breeze turned.

The sun came out on us, the shade blotches
went hazel: we heard names
bubble like stock-doves over the woods

as jockeys in stained silks gentled
those sweat-dark, shuddering horses
down to the walk.

The hard-hearted husband

'Has she gone then?' they asked,
stepping round the back of the house
whose cat skulked in the grass.

She'd left pegs dropped in the bean-row,
and a mauve terrycloth babygrow
stirred on the line as I passed.

Her damsons were ripe and her sage was in flower,
her roses tilted from last night's downpour,
her sweetpeas and sunflowers leaned anywhere.

'She got sick of it, then,' they guessed,
and wondered if the torn-up paper
might be worth reading, might be a letter.

'It was the bills got her,' they knew,
seeing brown envelopes sheafed with the white
in a jar on the curtainless windowsill,

some of them sealed still, as if she was through
with trying to pay, and would sit, chilled,
ruffling and arranging them like flowers
in the long dusks while the kids slept upstairs.

The plaster was thick with her shadows,
damp and ready to show
how she lived there and lay fallow

and how she stood at her window
and watched tall pylons stride down the slope
sizzling faintly, stepping away
as she now suddenly goes,

too stubborn to be ghosted at thirty.
She will not haunt here. She picks up her dirty
warm children and takes them

down to the gate which she lifts as it whines
and sets going a thin cry in her.
He was hard-hearted and no good to her
they say now, grasping the chance to be kind.

The haunting at Epworth

Epworth Rectory was the childhood home of John Wesley. In December 1716 the house was possessed by a poltergeist; after many unsuccessful attempts at exorcism the spirit, nicknamed 'Old Jeffery' by the little Wesley girls, left of its own accord.

Old Jeffery begins his night music.
The girls, sheathed in their brick skin,
giggle with terror. The boys are all gone
out to the world, 'continually sinning',
their graces exotic and paid for.

Old Jeffery rummages pitchforks
up the back chimney. The girls
open the doors to troops of exorcists
who plod back over the Isle of Axeholme
balked by the house. The scrimmage
of iron, shattering windows, and brickwork
chipped away daily is birdsong
morning and evening, or sunlight
into their unsunned lives.

Old Jeffery tires of the house slowly.
He knocks the back of the connubial bed
where nineteen Wesleys, engendered in artlessness
swarm, little ghosts of themselves.
The girls learn to whistle his music.

The house bangs like a side-drum
as Old Jeffery goes out of it. Daughters
in white wrappers mount to the windows, sons
coming from school make notes – the wildness
goes out towards Epworth and leaves nothing
but the bald house straining on tiptoe
after its ghost.

The bride's nights in a strange village

At three in the morning
while mist limps between houses
while cloaks and blankets
dampen with dew

the bride sleeps with her husband
bundled in a red blanket,
her mouth parts and a bubble
of sour breathing goes free.
She humps wool up to her ears
while her husband tightens his arms
and rocks her, mumbling. Neither awakes.

In the second month of the marriage
the bride wakes after midnight.
Damp-bodied
she lunges from sleep
hair pricking with sweat
breath knocking her sides.
She eels from her husband's grip
and crouches, listening.

The night is enlarged by sounds.
The rain has started.
It threshes leaves secretively
and there in the blackness
of whining dogs it finds out the house.
Its hiss enfolds her, blots up
her skin, then sifts off, whispering
in her like mirrors
the length of the rainy village.

Missile launcher passing at night

The soft fields part in hedges, each
binds each, copse pleats
rib up the hillside.

Darkness is coming and grass
bends downward.
The cattle out all night
eat, knee-deep, invisible
unless a headlight arcs on their mild faces.

The night's damp fastens, droplet by droplet,
onto the animals.
They vibrate to the passing of a missile launcher and stir
their patient eyelashes.

A blackbird
startled by floodlights
reproduces morning.

Cattle grids tremble and clang,
boots scrape
holly bursts against wet walls
lost at the moment of happening.

The marshalling yard

In the goods yard the tracks are unmarked.
Snow lies, the sky is full of it.
Its hush swells in the dark.

Grasped by black ice on black
a massive noise of breathing
fills the tracks;

cold women, ready for departure
smooth their worn skirts
and ice steals through their hands like children
from whose touch they have already been parted.

Now like a summer
the train comes
beating the platform
with its blue wings.

The women stir. They sigh.
Feet slide
warm on a wooden stairway
then a voice calls and
milk drenched with aniseed
drawls on the walk to school.

At last they leave.
Their breathless neighbours
steal from the woods, the barns,
and tender straw
sticks to their palms.

A cow here in the June meadow

A cow here in the June meadow
where clouds pile, tower above tower.

We lie, buried in sunburn,
our picnic a warm
paper of street tastes,

she like a gold cloud
steps, moony.
Her silky rump dips
into the grasses, buffeting
a mass of seed ready to run off in flower.

We stroll under the elder, smell
wine, trace blackfly along its leaf-veins

then burning and yawning we pile
kisses onto the hot upholstery.

Now evening shivers along the water surface.
The cow, suddenly planted, stands – her tender
skin pollened all over –
ready to nudge all night at the cold grasses,
her udder heavily and more heavily swinging.

Breakfast

Often when the bread tin is empty
and there's no more money for the fire
I think of you, and the breakfast you laid for me
– black bread and honey and beer.

I threw out a panful of wine yesterday –
the aluminium had turned it sour –
I have two colours of bread to choose from,
I'd take the white if I were poor,

so indigence is distant as my hands
stiff in unheated washing water,
but you, with your generous gift of butter
and cheese with poppy seeds, all in one morning meal

have drawn the blinds up at the bedside window
and I can watch the ships' tall masts appear.

Patrick I

Patrick, I cannot write
such poems for you as a father might
coming upon your smile,

your mouth, half sucking, half sleeping,
your tears shaken from your eyes like sparklers
break up the nightless weeks of your life:

lightheaded, I go to the kitchen
and cook breakfast, aching as you grow hungry.
Mornings are plain as the pages
of books in sedentary schooldays.

If I were eighty and lived next door
hanging my pale chemises on the porch
would I envy or pity my neighbour?

Polished and still as driftwood
she stands smoothing her dahlias;

liquid, leaking,
I cup the baby's head to my shoulder:

the child's a boy and will not share
one day these obstinate, exhausted mornings.

The apple fall

In a back garden I'm painting
the outside toilet in shell and antelope.
The big domestic Bramley tree
hangs close to me, rosy and leafless.
Sometimes an apple thumps
into the bushes I've spattered with turpentine
while my brush moves with a suck
over the burnt-off door frame.

Towels from the massage parlour
are out on the line next door:
all those bodies sweating into them
each day – the fabric stiffening –
towels bodiless and sex over.

I load the brush with paint again
and I hear myself breathing.
Sun slips off the wall
so the yard is cool
and lumbered with shadows,

and then a cannonade of apples
punches the wall and my arms,
the ripe stripes on their cheeks fall open,
flesh spurts and the juices fizz and glisten.

The plum tree

The plum was my parents' tree,
above them
as I was at my bedroom window
wondering why they chose to walk this way quietly
under the plum tree.

My sisters and I stopped playing
as they reached up and felt for the fruit.
It lay among bunches of leaves,
oval and oozing resin
out into pearls of gum.
They bit into the plums
without once glancing
back at the house.

Some years were thin:
white mildew streaking the trunk,
fruit buckled and green,

but one April
the tree broke from its temperate blossoming
and by late summer the branches
trailed earth, heavy with pound
after pound of bursting Victorias,

and I remember the oblivious steps
my parents took as they went quietly
out of the house one summer evening
to stand under the plum tree.

One yellow chicken

One yellow chicken
she picks up expertly and not untenderly
from the conveyor of chickens.

Its soft beak gobbles feverishly
at a clear liquid which might be
a dose of sugar-drenched serum –

the beak's flexible membrane
seems to engulf the chicken
as it tries to fix on the dropper's glass tip.

Clear yellow juice gulps through a tube
and a few drops, suddenly colourless,
swill round a gape wide as the brim of a glass

but the chicken doesn't seem afraid –
or only this much, only for this long
until the lab assistant flicks it back on
to the slowly moving conveyor of chickens
and it tumbles, catches itself,
then buoyed up by the rest
reels out of sight, cheeping.

Safe period

Your dry voice from the centre of the bed
asks 'Is it safe?'

and I answer for the days as if I owned them.
Practised at counting, I rock
the two halves of the month like a cradle.

The days slip over their stile
and expect nothing. They are just days,

and we're at it again, thwarting
souls from the bodies they crave.

They'd love to get into this room
under the yellow counterpane
we've torn to make a child's cuddly,

they'd love to slide into the sheets
between soft, much-washed
flannelette fleece,

they'd love to be here in the moulded spaces
between us, where there is no room,

but we don't let them. They fly about gustily,
noisy as our own children.

Sisters leaving before the dance

Sisters leaving before the dance,
before the caller gets drunk
or the yellow streamers unreel
looping like ribbons
here and there on the hair of the dancers,

sisters at the turn of the stairs
as the sound system
one-twos, as the squeezebox
mewed in its case

is slapped into breath, and that scrape
of the tables shoved back for the dance
burns like the strike of a match
in the cup of two hands.
Ripe melons and meat

mix in the binbags with cake
puddled in cherry-slime, wind
heavy with tar
blows back the yard door, and I'm

caught with three drinks in my hands
on the stairs looking up
at the sisters leaving before the dance,
not wishing to push past them
in their white broderie anglaise and hemmed

skirts civilly drawn
to their sides to make room
for the big men in suits,
and the girls in cerise

dance-slippers and cross-backed dresses
who lead the way up
and take charge of the tickets, and yet
from their lips canteloupe
fans as they speak

in bright quick murmurs between
a violin ghosting a tune
and the kids in the bar downstairs
begging for Coke, peaky but certain.

The sisters say their *good nights*
and all the while people stay bunched
on the stairs going up, showing respect
for the small words of the ones leaving,
the ones who don't stay for the dancing.

One sister twists a white candle
waxed in a nest of hydrangeas –
brick-red and uncommon, flowers
she really can't want – she bruises the limp

warm petals with crisp fingers
and then poises her sandal
over the next non-slip stair
so the dance streams at her heels
in the light of a half-shut door.

The dream-life of priests

Do they wake careless and warm
with light on the unwashed windows
and a perpetual smell of bacon,

do their hearts sink at today's martyr
with his unpronounceable name
and strange manner of execution?

Do they wake out of the darkness
with hearts thudding like ours
and reach for the souvenir lamp-switch

then shove a chair against the door
and key facts into the desk-top computer
while cold rattles along the corridor?

Do they cry out in sleep
at some barely-crushed thought,
some failure to see the joke,

or do they rest in their dreams
along the surface of the water
like a bevy of dragonflies

slack and blue in the shallows
whirring among reed-mace and water-forget-me-not
while the ripples cluck?

Do they wake in ordinary time
to green curtains slapping the frame
of a day that'll cloud later on,

to cars nudging and growling for space,
to a baptismal mother, wan with her eagerness
and her sleepless, milk-sodden nights?

Do they reach and stroke the uneven plaster
and sniff the lime-blossom threading
like silk through the room,

or do they wait, stretched out like babies
in the gold of its being too early
with sun on their ceilings wobbling like jelly

while their housekeepers jingle the milk-bottles
and cry 'Father!' in sixty-year-old voices
and scorch toast with devotion –

do they sense the milk in the pan rising
then dive with their blue chins, blundering
through prayer under their honeycomb blankets?

The parachute packers

The parachute packers with white faces
swathed over with sleep
and the stale bodily smell of sheets

make haste to tin huts where a twelve-hour
shift starts in ten minutes.
Their bare legs pump bicycle pedals,
they clatter on wooden-soled sandals
into the dazzling light over the work benches.

They rub in today's issue of hand-cream.
Their fingers skim on the silk
as the unwieldy billows of parachute flatten
like sea-waves, oiled, folded in sevens.

The only silk to be had
comes in a military packaging:
dull-green, printed, discreet,
gone into fashioning parachutes
to be wondered at like the flowers'
down-spinning, seed-bearing canopies
lodged in the silt of village memory.

A girl pulling swedes in a field
senses the shadow of parachutes
and gapes up, knees braced
and hair tangling. She must be riddled,
her warm juices all spilled
for looking upwards too early
into the dawn, leafy with parachutes.

Heavenly wide canopies
bring down stolid chaps with their rifle butts

ready to crack, with papers
to govern the upturned land,
with boots, barbed wire and lists on fine paper
thousands of names long.

I look up now at two seagulls,
at cloud drifts and a lamppost
bent like a feeding swan,

and at the sound of needles
seaming up parachutes in Nissen huts
with a hiss and pull through the stuff
of these celestial ball-dresses

for nuns, agents, snow-on-the-boots men
sewn into a flower's corolla
to the music of Workers' Playtime.

At dusk the parachute packers
release their hair from its nets
and ride down lanes whitened by cow-parsley
to village halls, where the dances
and beer and the first cigarettes
expunge the clouds of parachute silk
and rules touching their hair and flesh.

In the bar they're the girls who pack parachutes
for our boys. They can forget
the coughs of the guard on duty,
the boredom and long hours
and half-heard cries of caught parachutists.

Privacy of rain

Rain. A plump splash
on tense, bare skin.
Rain. All the May leaves
run upward, shaking.

Rain. A first touch
at the nape of the neck.
Sharp drops kick the dust, white
downpours shudder
like curtains, rinsing
tight hairdos to innocence.

I love the privacy of rain,
the way it makes things happen
on verandahs, under canopies
or in the shelter of trees
as a door slams and a girl runs out
into the black-wet leaves.
By the brick wall an iris
sucks up the rain
like intricate food, its tongue
sherbetty, furred.

Rain. All the May leaves
run upward, shaking.
On the street bud-silt
covers the windscreens.

Pilgrims

Let us think that we are pilgrims
in furs on this bleak water.
The Titanic's lamps hang on its sides like fruit
on lit cliffs. We're shriven for rescue.

The sea snaps at our caulking.
We bend to our oars and praise God
and flex our fingers to bring
a drowned child out from the tarpaulin.

We're neither mothers nor fathers, but children,
fearful and full of trust,
lamblike as the Titanic goes down
entombing its witnesses.

We row on in a state of grace
in our half-empty lifeboats, sailing
westward for America, pilgrims,
numb to the summer-like choir
of fifteen hundred companions.

When you've got

When you've got the plan of your life
matched to the time it will take
but you just want to press SHIFT/BREAK
and print over and over
this is not what I was after
this is not what I was after,

when you've finally stripped out the house
with its iron-cold fireplace,
its mouldings, its mortgage,
its single-skin walls
but you want to write in the plaster
'This is not what I was after,'

when you've got the rainbow-clad baby
in his state-of-the-art pushchair
but he arches his back at you
and pulps his Activity Centre
and you just want to whisper
'This is not what I was after,'

when the vacuum seethes and whines in the lounge
and the waste-disposal unit blows,
when tenners settle in your account
like snow hitting a stove,
when you get a chat from your spouse
about marriage and personal growth,

when a wino comes to sleep in your porch
on your Citizen's Charter
and you know a hostel's opening soon
but your headache's closer
and you really just want to torch

the bundle of rages and newspaper

and you'll say to the newspaper
'This is not what we were after,
this is not what we were after.'

Those shady girls

Those shady girls on the green side of the street,
those far-from-green girls who keep to the shade,
those shady girls in mysterious suits
with their labels half-showing
as the cream flap of the jacket swings open,
those girls kicking aside the front-panelled pleats
of their cream suits with cerise lapels,

those on-coming girls,
those girls swinging pearly umbrellas
as tightly-sheathed as tulips in bud
from an unscrupulous street-seller,
those girls in cream and cerise suits
which mark if you touch them,
those girls with their one-name appointments
who walk out of the sunshine.

Jo Shapcott

Hubei Province Tornado

Mrs Yang has experienced
an air adventure. The tornado
that uprooted trees lifted
the umbrella-holding woman
several hundred yards high
into the sky. She crossed
the Jiuda River. She was carried
for five hundred and fifty yards
then landed slowly. Strangely,
though she was injured by hailstones,
she was intact.

With the Big Tray

With the big tray
Hilary had to mind the tea service
at each end of the long march
up the staircase (those places
by the newel posts where her hips
had to angle and re-angle
at the new levels). Then
there was an impasse
at the bedroom door
where really another person was needed
to get a grip on the ebony handle.
In the event an elbow served
and after wriggling and clinking
round the door like a belly dancer
she found herself inside,
foolish on the Moroccan rug.
There had been an audience:
a housefly was swooping by the lilac
in mother's clover vase – the one
Nicholas had thrown for her.
The sun constructed an avenue
to the bedside table
and now the housefly played
boomerang in and out of the light.
Hilary surprised herself by breaking wind.
Secretly, her large smell
made her feel as real and salty
as a merchant adventurer
but she would take something for it
from the bathroom cabinet anyway.
She set the tray down by the bed

noting as she did the ornate little table.
It had been made by a local craftsman
and she had, at first, been impressed
by what she interpreted
as the mark of difficulty
that its execution had left on his face.
Now there were more or less
three white rings on the walnut veneer.

Lies

In reality, sheep are brave, enlightened
and sassy. They are walking clouds
and like clouds have forgotten
how to jump. As lambs they knew.
Lambs jump because in their innocence
they still find grass exciting.
Some turf is better for tiptoeing
say the lambs. Springy meadows
have curves which invite fits
of bouncing and heel-kicking
to turn flocks of lambs
into demented white spuds boiling in the pot.
Then there is a French style of being a lamb
which involves show and a special touch
at angling the bucking legs. Watch carefully
next time: Lambs love to demonstrate –
you won't have to inveigle.
Eventually, of course, lambs grow trousers
and a blast of wool
which keeps them anchored to the sward.
Then grass is first and foremost
savoury, not palpable.
I prefer the grown sheep: even when damp
she is brave, enlightened and sassy,
her eye a kaleidoscope of hail and farewell,
her tail her most eloquent organ of gesture.
When she speaks, it is to tell me
that she is under a spell, polluted.
Her footwear has been stolen
and the earth rots her feet.
In reality she walks across the sky
upside-down in special pumps.

Through the pregnancy I can't remember a whine
from my mother; she gave up smoking, put alphabet
paper on the spare room walls, forbore to strike
my brother, tried not to smoke, nor breathe in smog.
That's the sort of thing which puts an obligation
on you. She risks her life, she suffers;
it's all up for friendship or equality: your guilt
goes whizzing like a satellite.

                But it still
wasn't wrong to be born in 1953 (though it was a myopic
year, full of the coronation illusion). My mum
held me up at the hospital window to see the great
procession, so she said. She admired the true
beauty of the Queen and her courage so soon
after the old King died.

                    My mum had a bully
of an illness after I was born, went home to no
carpet and an urgency to go back to work.
I went too in 1953, under her arm like a book.
Teachers were scarce; it was a small defect
to go along with a new baby, the prize
that was soon to become myself.

Birthday Surprise

As Daddy straightened the last candle
his thumb smudged the blue icing-sugar seven:
I opened my mouth wide to scream.
But the surprise of a trickle down my leg
killed the noise. 'Power!' I was thinking.
'A puddle on the rug.' Then Mother
got out a tissue and blotted the wet shape
so carefully mapped and steaming on the Wilton –
my Florida, my Amazon, my Indies.

Venus Observes Herself

Her smile
makes her feel prickly –
it's lopsided like a guitar:
she wants rid of that half-curve
which seems puffy to her touch.

Her way would be clear to seventh
Heaven if she could master
this art of arriving on shells
with poise
and a waist.

She's working towards
an increase in breast/nipple ratio,
an imperceptible up-tilt
which would balance the economy
of her happinesses, cut
into her griefs like a science,
secure her potential like a frame.

Now she rises:
the shell razes the water –
the Seasons advance clenching garments.

The Mug

The mug is cast in earthenware
and coloured like pale stone, the usual shade
for mixing eggs, drinking or watering plants.

Around it, in dark brown, some people stroll –
Egyptians? – all in profile looking right
(though there is one who's facing widdershins
but slightly turned, as though about to follow
the others' lead). Some bend to long curved jars;
one raises something, one holds out papyrus
with a smooth arm. These gyral figures share
the same suggestion of a slight breast's curve;
the same androgynous hips; the same blunt hair;
the knotted cloth around the waist, the same.

The handle has a bite snapped from its arc
where you can see the clay in cross-section.
It's not so bad – you can still pick it up
by bridging the brief gap with three tight knuckles
and hanging on, with your thumb and little finger,
firm as a flying buttress, for dear life.

Inside the mug the rings of tea show brown
against the stone – as if to demonstrate
age to an expert, like the rings through logs
or at the ivory base of a whale's tooth.

Station Bookstand

Although the platform seems flat
it is only a disguise
for a curvy being with
thoughts you must conjure in
your own additions to this
poem. All the images
can revolve on the bookstand.
You dream you're the narrator
in a tale where they couple
in fours, and yet another
flagellant offers himself
for a spell of harm. Meanwhile
in another paperback
the heroine's manacled
to the bedpost again and,
of course, her long back arches
up from the leopard-skin spread.
Think of it, millions of us
nudes, spies, leather ladies, studs
and hoods stationed all along
the hissing tracks of England.

Love in the Lab

One day
the technicians
touched souls

as they exchanged
everyday noises
above the pipette.

Then they knew
that the state of molecules
was not humdrum.

The inscriptions
on the specimen jars
which lined the room in racks
took fire in their minds:

what were yesterday
mere hieroglyphs
from the periodic table

became today urgent proof
that even here –
laboratory life –
writing is mystical.

The jars glinted under their labels:
it had taken fifteen years
to collect and collate them.

Now the pair were of one mind.
Quietly, methodically
they removed the labels
from each of the thousands
of jars. It took all night.

At dawn, rows of bare glass
winked at their exhausted coupling
against the fume cupboard.

Using their white coats
as a disguise
they took their places at the bench
and waited for the morning shift.

Fun with Robert and Elizabeth

Sitting down in the draught was distracting.
It was distracting in itself to have
to stay with cousins when you went away;
their house was too close to the thoroughfare.
Even now the troops passed on their march
by the window, having to adhere
to the autumn training routine designed to make
men of granite: bones, skin, muscles
and every item in the kitbag stone.
But distraction could be fun with Robert
and Elizabeth laughing at the simplest jokes
about the things to be seen through the window,
chuckling at the rich sounds from outside.
Towards lunchtime they would become more terse,
each listening to interpret the faint sounds
of the other's scourings on the paper.

Elizabeth Looks at Robert

For a woman to hang down her head like a lily through life, and 'die of
a rose in aromatic pain' at her death, – to sit or lounge as in a Book of
Beauty, and be 'defended' by the strong and mighty thinkers on all sides
of her – this, he thinks, is her destiny and glory.
                    [Elizabeth Barrett, Letter to Miss Mitford, February 1845]

Terminology was a science she wasn't at all sure of.
She suspected that Robert, more political animal,
proudly bristling his resilient epidermis
would have moved with confidence
at the court of Terminus, rare god of boundaries.
She eyed him cautiously on the other sofa:
yes – cantankerous, but certainly comfortable.
He could parse anything and was a fiend
with crosswords. She sucked her pen thoughtfully
surprising the ailing clockwork in her chest
into another cough. Her lungs
felt like a pair of rotting bellows
in a smithy where the strange conjunction
of heat, flesh, metal, moisture and noise
had made the leather crack unbearably
where the air pressed on the seams.

Robert in the Kitchen in the Dark

Of course these things are not *mine*. I think they are usually spoken of as
ours, that tea bag of a word which steeps in the conditional.
[Elizabeth Hardwick, *Sleepless Nights*]

Stepping in here means the end of carpet.
My leading toe locates a tiny lake
next to the sink. At least it *was* my toe
but now I hear and feel a clammy trout
flap sadly in the shallows. Happiness,
I suddenly perceive, is only dry.
My life's a foreign mountain, so uphill,
translating fuzzy shapes into familiars:
I ought to know my teapot, but a scarf
of blurry grey wraps it entirely round.
My memory knows it to be red and slowly,
now I'm staring really hard, I see
faint pink ebb into it and then recede,
a welcome spurt of paint into the dark.
Aboard the drainer, propped in open pose,
the tilted biscuit tin's an obscure helmet,
vague heart for Elizabeth, mucky continent.

Yesterday Was Elizabeth's Turn to Cook

It certainly hasn't the drama of: I saw the old, white-bearded frigate master on the dock and signed up for the journey. But after all, 'I' am a woman.

[Elizabeth Hardwick, *Sleepless Nights*]

My hair rose a little in the heat
from the lit rings every time
I leaned over the gas. This was
a pose to serve for bowing modestly
to a warm public, but in this setting
more cinematic than theatrical,
framed by the eye level grill just so.
Only chopped onions were in the pan,
the muscles in the face not quite tense,
but not relaxed. The upward movement
of my hair in the heat tickled through
the scalp into the skull and, it seemed,
released the smell of every separate
warmed shaft into the frying air.
I get them mixed up, the warmth
and the heat — and where I feel which:
in my hair, along my arms, at the throat.

Robert Watches Elizabeth Knitting

It will be found that DNA mentions nothing but relations . . . The relata,
the end components of the relationships in the corporeal world, are
perhaps never mentioned.

[Gregory Bateson, *Mind and Nature*]

Knitting is a bore but Elizabeth
nods and smiles and clicks to herself
as though it were more than just useful.
She goes happily about the task,
moving in and out of it without haste,
perfecting tension, cabling, ribs.
She looks forward to the sewing-up
but not too much, knowing how to mesh
the pleasure of the final thing,
all sensuality and wholeness,
with the independent life of every stitch.

Where does it come from, this compulsion
to call her a whole list of things
other than what she is? The string-winder,
the long-fingered, the sitting clock,
the fur-maker and on and on and on.
From shanks by sharp shears to Shape Shoulders
she is what she is, my hank-shifter,
the one who weaves and stitches up wool.

The needles click in a rhythm I can't get at:
part and whole, part and whole;
two heartbeats, a breath, two heartbeats.
Her lips silently move to mark
the four or five last stitches in the line.

Elizabeth's pattern is cut small
and pasted in her diary: a book of days,
a book of stitches; lunch-dates and meetings,
Right Border and Neckband, Left Front.
There is no picture, only the long strings
of phonemes – purls and plains
made unpronounceable by the feminine science
of the knitting pattern. She bows
her head to translate the printed page
into this odd manipulation of sticks and string.

I can't get my mind round knitting.
It starts to have everything
when you come down to it – rhythm,
colour and slow but perceptible change.
The meaning is all in the gaps:
a pattern of holes marked out by woolly colour,
a jumper made of space, division and relations.

Strange to see these youngish hands,
with no puffiness or obvious veins,
repeat the banal and tiny motions
over days over weeks over months.
I ask too much and am too hasty;
this knitting is an exercise in trust.

Robert and Elizabeth Sit Down Again

I was then a 'we'.
[Elizabeth Hardwick]

This was a sudden break from plain routine
as much a surprise as a new baby's strong grasp
or a rake's late notion for the church.
Elizabeth and Robert had not sat down
to write together with the big watch
between them on the deal table,
since that tour of the fells seven years ago
when Robert had been much taken
with a remarkable and fine style of bootrack
which they had chanced on at an inn.
Ah, the heady days, with minds in utter engagement,
mouths distorted in an ache of mutual beaming.
But now this too was important,
new and pleasurable like an unexpected jink
in a straight path, or a glimpse of a fresh shade
of pink in a spectrum grown dull.
So much for the sitting down; now for the matter.

Tom and Jerry Visit England

O boy, I thought. A chance
to visit England and O boy here, out
of nowhere, a voice to describe it. Reader,
I dreamt of coming back to tell you how I marched
round the Tower of London, in a beefeater suit,
swished my axe at Jerry, belted after him
into the Bloody Tower, my back legs
circling like windmills in a gale
while ravens flapped around our heads.
You would hear it all: tea with the Queen
at Buckingham Palace and me scattering
the cucumber sandwiches at the sight
of Jerry by the silver salver. I couldn't wait
for the gorgeous tableau: Queenie with her mouth
in a little shocked screaming shape, her crown
gone crooked as she stood cringing on the throne
with her skirts up round her knees, and Jerry
down there laughing by the footstool.
I would be a concertina zig-zag by that time
with a bone china cup stuffed in my face
and a floral teapot shoved on my head so hard
my brains would form a spout and a handle
when it cracked and dropped off.

I can't get this new voice to explain to you
the ecstasy in the body when you fling
yourself into such mayhem, open yourself
to any shape at all and able to throw out
stars of pain for everyone to see.

But reader, the visit wasn't like that.
I ended up in a poem and it made me uneasy.

Cats prefer to skulk and sulk
in the dark, we prefer mystery
and slinking. This is even true of me
with my stupid human face opening
into only two or three stupid expressions:
cunning, surprise and maybe rage.
And I couldn't find Jerry.
'Where's the mouse?' I tripped
over commas and colons hard like diamonds, looking
for him. 'Where's the mouse?' I kept asking,
'Where's the mouse?' I banged full face into a query –
and ended up with my front shaped
like a question mark for hours. That was scary:
I usually pop right back into myself in seconds.
So I hesitated for once before flinging myself
down the bumpy staircase where all the lines ended.
I went on my rear and at the bottom you would have seen
    me,
end up, bristling with splinters, and nose down
snuffling for any trace of mouse smell.
Reader, it was my first tragic movie:
I couldn't find the mouse.

Superman Sounds Depressed

Nothing could have prepared me for this life
in which it all hinges on me,

where it's only me and my past now left
to reassure the world. The trouble is

they forget me fast and start counting
on krill, or thinking they understand

turbulence: so I have to make regular
appearances on the borders

of disaster, dropping through some backdoor
in space whenever I feel the gravity

of their need. Apples for the teacher
are all I get for it, for holding the railway

train on the high viaduct by a single joint
of my little finger, for blowing hard

at the last moment to keep the water upright
in the shape of the shattered dam, for stopping

a model of the earth based on real chaos from
breaking through. I feel spelled all wrong,

stuck in the east wind
with my face caught in an expression

which would mean world financial crisis
if the president wore it. Give me dinner,

a lovely long dinner in dim light, with someone,
someone who will propose something rude

so it doesn't sound rude – just delicious –
nothing personal, anxious or brutal about it

though it might seem all of those things
to others when it's not night, over their ordinary

sandwiches: wholemeal, mustard
and fragile morsels. My head aches; I want

that woman and enough passion to blast away
any hope of understanding what's happening

to me. And I want us to eat scallops,
and I want to lick the juice from her chin

as though I could save the world that way,
and I won't even ask what passion is for.

Goat

Dusk, deserted road, and suddenly
I was a goat. To be truthful, it took
two minutes, though it seemed sudden,
for the horns to pop out of my skull,
for the spine to revolutionize and go
horizontal, for the fingers to glue
together and for the nails to become
important enough to upgrade to hoof.
The road was not deserted any more, but full
of goats, and I liked that, even though I hate
the rush hour on the tube, the press of bodies.
Now I loved snuffling behind his or her ear,
licking a flank or two, licking and snuffling here,
there, wherever I liked. I lived for the push
of goat muscle and goat bone, the smell of goat fur,
goat breath and goat sex. I ended up on the edge
of the crowd where the road met the high
hedgerow with the scent of earth, a thousand
kinds of grass, leaves and twigs, flower-heads
and the intoxicating tang of the odd ring-pull
or rubber to spice the mixture. I wanted
to eat everything. I could have eaten the world
and closed my eyes to nibble at the high
sweet leaves against the sunset. I tasted
that old sun and the few dark clouds
and some tall buildings far away in the next town.
I think I must have swallowed an office block
because this grinding enormous digestion tells me
it's stuck on an empty corridor which has
at the far end, I know, a tiny human figure.

Love Song with a Flock of Sheep

'Win a flock of sheep' said the advertisement.
'Sheep Dip: an eight year old pure malt whisky.
You will find an entry form on every bottle.'

I will. I will buy the whisky,
I will find the entry form. I will:
I will win the sheep and I'll give them to you.

Keep the flock at home
and let them graze around the house.
Kindly and damp, they'll eat the carpet
and will start on the wallpaper too,
your interior decorations will be masticated away.
The flock is softer than soft furnishings
but when they've eaten all that they'll start
on the hard stuff. They'll munch their way
through the mantelpiece and everything –
your books, your manuscripts –
will fly into their placid mouths.

I know you. You'll like it better without
all that ruminated stuff. You want
the woolly life, carding and spinning,
with only sheep for furniture and bedclothes.
The flock will find you out eventually
and start their blowing in your ears
and their nuzzling across your hair.
It will begin in the kitchen with a fleecy
brush along the backs of your knees.
They'll surround you on the sofa
and drink out of your bath. Your clothes
will go into the three stomachs and in the dark

you'll feel sheep nibble between your toes
and suck your toenails. They will graze
your legs, removing every hair with teeth
so precise and shy you'll feel only
a mist of breath and lips. They'll move
in a cloud across your chest, your belly,
face and beard – everywhere – cropped
down to a downy stubble, peaceful as pasture.
Soon you will be as shorn as a yearling lamb
and twice as happy, blissoming with the flock.

When I arrive, dressed as Bo-Peep,
I won't get a look in. But by hook or by crook
you shall have them anyway: sheep fleecy, sheep shorn
and me lovelorn.

Vegetable Love

I'd like to say the fridge
was clean, but look at the rusty
streaks down the back wall
and the dusty brown pools
underneath the salad crisper.

And this is where I've lived
the past two weeks, since I was pulled
from the vegetable garden.
I'm wild for him: I want to stay crunchy
enough to madden his hard palate and his tongue,
every sensitive part inside his mouth.
But almost hour by hour now, it seems,
I can feel my outer leaves losing resistance,
as oxygen leaks in, water leaks out
and the same tendency creeps further
and further towards my heart.

Down here there's not much action,
just me and another, even limper, lettuce
and half an onion. The door opens so many,
so many times a day, but he never looks
in the salad drawer where I'm curled in a corner.

There's an awful lot of meat. Strange cuts:
whole limbs with their grubby hair,
wings and thighs of large birds,
claws and beaks. New juice
gathers pungency as it rolls down
through the smelly strata of the refrigerator,
and drips on to our fading heads.

The thermostat is kept as low as it will go,
and when the weather changes
for the worse, what's nearest
to the bottom of the fridge starts to freeze.
Three times we've had cold snaps,
and I've felt the terrifying pain
as ice crystals formed at my fringes.

Insulation isn't everything in here:
you've got to relax into the cold,
let it in at every pore. It's proper
for food preservation. But I heat up
again at the thought of him,
at the thought of mixing into one juice
with his saliva, of passing down his throat
and being ingested with the rest
into his body cells where I'll learn
by osmosis another lovely version
of curl, then shrivel, then open again to desire.

I'm Contemplated by a Portrait of a Divine

I cannot speak to you. My lips are fused
where an archangel kissed them. I have never
made much of myself although I know,
sometimes, that space is touching me
because I have seen the crack in the universe
through which the galaxies stream. O God,
I will always know how to walk, no rest, until
it just ends in blackness when I fall down flat.
I have one arching eyebrow: my whole life
is in that eyebrow where an angel nestles
at the root of every hair, raising it up.
Dear Christ. I can hear vice rushing through
the grass. There is someone here.
If I could lick the glass clean
from this side, I might see her, though
I already know she would look the way
I want my soul to look. This pose
which I strain to keep, in which I lean
on the desk for dear life, is not a pose.
It's so important for keeping the drawer shut
in case my heart should slip out, fly up.

Matter

He touched my skin
all afternoon
as though he could feel
the smallest particles
which make me up.

By tea time he knew each
of the billions of electrons
which fly through my body
every second.

Then I think he was searching
for the particles
not yet discovered
but believed to exist.

Then I didn't know
what time it was any more
and neither of us knew
which was inside or outside
as he reached somewhere
very deep and fingered gold –
charms, stranges, tops and gravitons –
but not the words he wanted
which only come now.

Muse

When I kiss you in all the folding places
of your body, you make that noise like a dog
dreaming, dreaming of the long runs he makes
in answer to some jolt to his hormones,
running across landfills, running, running
by tips and shorelines from the scent of too much,
but still going with head up and snout
in the air because he loves it all
and has to get away. I have to kiss deeper
and more slowly – your neck, your inner arm,
the neat creases under your toes, the shadow
behind your knee, the white angles of your groin –
until you fall quiet because only then
can I get the damned words to come into my mouth.

Phrase Book

I'm standing here inside my skin,
which will do for a Human Remains Pouch
for the moment. Look down there (up here).
Quickly. Slowly. This is my own front room

where I'm lost in the action, live from a war,
on screen. I am an Englishwoman, I don't understand you.
What's the matter? You are right. You are wrong.
Things are going well (badly). Am I disturbing you?

TV is showing bliss as taught to pilots:
Blend, Low silhouette, Irregular shape, Small,
Secluded. (Please write it down. Please speak slowly.)
Bliss is how it was in this very room

when I raised my body to his mouth,
when he even balanced me in the air,
or at least I thought so and yes the pilots say
yes they have caught it through the Side-Looking

Airborne Radar, and through the J-Stars.
I am expecting a gentleman (a young gentleman,
two gentlemen, some gentlemen). Please send him
(them) up at once. This is really beautiful.

Yes they have seen us, the pilots, in the Kill Box
on their screens, and played the routine for
getting us Stealthed, that is, Cleansed, to you and me,
Taken Out. They know how to move into a single room

like that, to send in with Pinpoint Accuracy, a hundred
    Harms.
I have two cases and a cardboard box. There is another
bag there. I cannot open my case – look out,
the lock is broken. Have I done enough?

Bliss, the pilots say, is for evasion
and escape. What's love in all this debris?
Just one person pounding another into dust,
into dust. I do not know the word for it yet.

Where is the British Consulate? Please explain.
What does it mean? What must I do? Where
can I find? What have I done? I have done
nothing. Let me pass please. I am an Englishwoman.

from THE WINDOWS
after Rilke

Jetzt wär es Zeit, das Götter träten aus bewohnten Dingen . . .
(Now it is time that gods came walking out of lived-in
    things . . .)

— Rainer Maria Rilke

I

It's enough that all the things
around are more real than anything else,
more real than me. The furniture, balcony,
doors, the windows, I spoke to them
and they talked back.

Then a woman, shy, came into the picture
and the windows flattened back into the walls,
the bits of furniture sat down again on the carpet.
Her arms, hair, smell made the dead things
quiet again, but I knew I would lose her too.

IV

It's true, I do talk to you more
when I'm drunk, the chair pulled up close,
my forehead and the glass in my hand
pressed against the pane.

My nose is so
close up I can see
the separate pores
as drops on the surface.

So there's me, my face at least,
but all the time the shadow
of something else, the dirt
on the glass, the big mess outside.

VI

I do want love deep down, somewhere in the back
of my spine.
I watch the window now as if she were a woman
stretching the stars
into dawn, everything a lover must know.
She's mean,
early on, but I like that, it gets me ready
for the sun's explosion
when my eyes don't know what to do
with all that
after the different abandon of the night.

Maybe there's nothing there after all
except the air
but I'm sure the sky must be made of more,
the way the birds
seem to hold on to it, the way they move
their feathers,
the way they measure it, taste it, fuck it
as they fly.

IX

O boo hoo, O shame.
Window, your skin's wet inside
from my tears and wet
outside with rain.

We've got this close
too late, too soon;
now I'm dressed up in curtains,
voile, organdy, void.

XI

I can't help it, I taste
whatever you have to offer.
You taste of night and day.
You taste of all the weathers.

Maybe that's everything, maybe
nothing, all show for the eyes
keeping me awake in case
I miss something wonderful.

Promises, promises; and all the while
the world shrivels in front of me.
I'm tired and still my eyes gobble roses
rainforests, oceans, satellites, the moon.

XIV

I'm a sod in the morning, and so are you, sky
up there, all square, mouthing things at me
and licking the room till it's worn out,
till it sticks out its tongue at you, in return:
two great liars wagging their tongues at each other –
then at me. And watch what you say about me,

or I'll beat you up, I'll beat all the bad tongues;
you say it again and again, you keep talking about
the fall, the rug, the dirty drop into bed.

XV

I'm just playing around, window,
fooling my own eyes and you
when I want so much to translate
us both up into the sky.

You've pulled out of me a final form
which comes through you or from you.
There's a crack in the corner
where the putty is loose.

I want to climb and see you
climb too into a new constellation.
You, window, and you, stars, and me,
I want us all to be rhymes.

The Mad Cow Talks Back

I'm not mad. It just seems that way
because I stagger and get a bit irritable.
There are wonderful holes in my brain
through which ideas from outside can travel
at top speed and through which voices,
sometimes whole people, speak to me
about the universe. Most brains are too
compressed. You need this spongy
generosity to let the others in.

I love the staggers. Suddenly the surface
of the world is ice and I'm a magnificent
skater turning and spinning across whole hard
Pacifics and Atlantics. It's risky when
you're good, so of course the legs go before,
behind, and to the side of the body from time
to time, and then there's the general embarrassing
collapse, but when that happens it's glorious
because it's always when you're travelling
most furiously in your mind. My brain's like
the hive: constant little murmurs from its cells
saying this is the way, this is the way to go.

Mad Cow Dance

I like to dance. Bang. I love to dance. Push.

It makes me savage and brilliant. Stomp. To
my own rhythm, rhythm. I lead or I don't

have a partner. No market for partners,
just this wide floor for the dance.
I think I was born here. Swoop. I don't care.

Even if I'd been born in the back of a car

the chassis and each blessed spring
would have jumped as I leapt out

of my mum. Up. Down to the ocean, perhaps
the beach? Hah. Stone steps and stone walls,
the pebbled strand, try to stall my special

high-kicks for the sea. But fireflies

know I'm here, raving with light,
they swirl down my spine. Swish. My tail

goes bam, thwack against the backs
of my legs. Pleasure, local pleasure.
Listen, sitting-down reader, I reckon

faces would be red if you knew what

was next. The little fibres
of my muscles give me such a charge.

Bread and butter. Release. Ceasefire
between my legs and my brain. Sweet oil
flows down to my little hooves. I like

to turn and call to my friends in

northern towns: kick out, kick back, fruity,
for a second. We can meet among characters

who don't dance, and hoof it till dawn, gas
on and on even when we're moving the most.
Four legs increase splits into splats,

just watch me

become
pure product, pure

use,
pure perfume,
jasmine and fucked.

Volumes

They put me in a fever. It's not enough
to look. I want to hold them all
and stuff them in the gaps in my head.
I gallop past Health towards Travel
where I break into a muck sweat
as I lift and sniff a book about Verona.
The odour makes me stagger and long
to be a book mite, to live right inside
and gulp holes through the picture maps.
I don't trust myself in Fiction. The thought
of those thousands and thousands of stories –
the crush and babble of other minds –
makes the whites of my eyes show and roll.
Last time I sauntered by those shelves
I slammed into the New Titles display
and crashed right through a pyramid of books
on to my back among the toppled photos
of authors winking at the carry on.
I got a cuppa and a pat on the rump
from the kind saleslady who has the bubble
of book hysteria herself, I'd guess.
If she could, she'd wear print on her skin.
There are words written for everything,
I think, and it's only a matter of time
before I find a new 'How To' book:
how to stand upright, how not to fall
and how not to cry out when you do.

The Mad Cow Tries to Write the Good Poem

The police came once when I was doing my death dance
to the amazing circular music which had entered a gap
near my cortex and acted as powerfully as a screwdriver
on my soul. I wove in and out of the green trees. I used
my hooves as gentle weapons in the air. A bit of newspaper
fame came my way that day, but shit, it was a performance
ephemeral, and certainly not the good poem. Lasting.
How can I last when I live in a shed and even
the postman doesn't know how to find me?
It's dark in here. Light would echo the gaps
in my brain coils and set off a fizzing reaction,
not so much pounding, more an explosion
followed by a flowing moment when the taboo
people arrive. They're dressed in red and
stand formally around my skull as though staged
for an opera. And when they sing – sometimes as many
as seven at once – then, friend, please, the good
poem is sounding all round this hut, my head, the world,
I hear it written in the streaky emulsion on the walls,
in my own messing on the floor, in the nation's smeary
    dailies,
in lovely people's ears, their breath, your breath:
it's new every time, always wanted and easy to spot
because I know what it looks like with my eyes closed.

A Walk in the Snow

There's something shameless about
snowfall, the way it lies there,
does nothing but changes everything.
So when freak storms hit London

I couldn't resist all that cleanness;
the glitter on the street outside
made me salivate, the dazzle
and glamour on our ordinary road.

I tottered out with Deirdre, sliding –
sliding worst of all where ice
was topped by snow. We hung on
to each other. I don't know who hung

more or hung on longer, while we rocked
with laughter and those sharp movements
the upper body makes to stay upright.
Breathless like that you talk too loudly,

as though the volume's been turned right up.
Everything's too big – the rhythm of your body
too large, too loud in the effort to keep
your torso pointed straight down the pavement,

your legs true to where you want to go.
We were heading for the park, and we made it,
but left ourselves too tired even to think
about the end. The helpless feeling made us laugh

until I fell on my back in the snow,
my breath, the laughter and the cold air
bursting in my chest as I lay there.
Sick, dizzy and squinting in the sunshine

I looked up to see a spread of branches
filled with frost, every twig cluttered
with wings, haloes, stars. Deirdre
plonked herself next to me and of course,

after we'd sat there we couldn't get up.
We had to roll over and over towards
the nearest tree, crawling the last part.
A stupid dog, the small sort, found us

and jumped and snuffled and yapped until I said,
'If the fucker would shut up, everybody
wouldn't see us.' We edged close enough
to the tree for Deirdre to pull herself up,

then she reached out for me. We were laughing
so hard water was running down our legs and I said,
'Deirdre, did you ever think we would come to this?'
And she said, 'No, never, never, never.'

The Mad Cow Believes She is the Spirit of the Weather

People out walking lean into the wind, the rain:
they believe it thwarts the weather to welcome it like that.
I can happily get lost for hours in a swirl of showers
because I was born into weather. They still tell
how my mother pushed me out of her body
on to a rock and I split the stone in two while the rain
washed me and the thunder broke overhead.
I was a junior cloud goddess, with storms following
me, winds and whirlwinds, shots of rain
and a split sky above my head. Always moving,
I kept one jump ahead of getting wet, kicking
back at the clouds with my hind legs
to keep them there. It's harder now, here
in the future: my brain has the characteristics
of a sponge and the rain seeps into the holes.
I think I'm making chaos. My vests
don't keep me warm and when I last sneezed
a volcano in the Pacific threw a sheet of dust
around the world. I'm dangerous to the earth.
I spat and a blanket of algae four miles long
bloomed on the Cornish coast. I rubbed
the sleep from my eyes and a meteor large enough
to make the earth wobble in its orbit
came very close indeed. I have been sad recently
and now the weather has changed for good.

Work in the City

Yes I do hold down a job and I find
the air in my brain helps combat
the stress. Once, carrying
my lunch back to the office, the tea
steaming in a polystyrene cup, the roll crunched
in a paper bag under my arm, the juggle
of food, briefcase, drink started to collapse.
It was around midday. I know the commuter
paths from the station, how to weave through
the concrete walkways, over roads in the spots
where traffic parts and lets you miraculously
through. These are the routes where the classic
people live, the ones who'll stick in my memory cells
even when the mind's shot, great blank slots of time
and visions revolving by turns like the movies.
They are the ones who ask me for everything
as I go by, every day, everything I have. One boy
leans against the wood palings he sleeps behind,
calling for change from his nest of blankets,
calling for my cup of tea, calling me love
as he crawls through the gap in the wood.
It's hard to stay perfect on that route, but
this day I was smiling at a lovely fantasy
until I slipped up on a piece of hamburger mashed
on the road, turning the juggle with my possessions
into a full stunt routine, legs, arms flying, the food
I was bound to waste at the end of it all. Then
the boy with the mad embroidery of muck
on his lapel stared me down again, daring me
to be bad. I offered him my apple and he turned
green, muttered, clasped his body in many places

and swung away. I sensed I was getting a tongue-lashing
and didn't want to ignore it, but I couldn't understand
a word. I put the food in a little pile in front of him,
the steaming tea, the papers, briefcase, all
the bags. I took off my coat, my shoes, every
piece of clothing and stood sweating in the light rain
but he didn't want me to know his language,
his eminence, his damnation or his delight.

Spaghetti Junction

after Hans Magnus Enzensberger

Ranting, belted up and bitter, if it's not the leather heated
seats, it's the stonking space frame chassis, the abuse
   overtaking
and all that knowing about insurance, scarce spare parts,
then the traffic jam, the blue light, the stretcher.

From below you're watching instruments wink, you're
   slanting
under the alternative light of the anaesthetic.
The sister's uniform is white; she's well into her TV.
   Headphones.
Dramas you can't hear flicker over her dark face.

A gear crunches in the brain. Rear-view mirror,
signal, manoeuvre but don't look now. Central locking.
Even screaming hurts. Little bubbles rise,
glass marbles, in the intravenous drip.

The traffic clears; you're really motoring. The double
wishbone independent suspension's a tad spongy but then
spring rates, bushing stiffnesses and geometries equal
roadholding fantastic. Everything's stereo, the drumroll,

stereo, heartbeat, the hiss of oxy-acetylene
cutting the ditched wreck open in blue, the pat, pat
of mud falling later, falling from the spade splat on
that place between cracked eyeballs where your spectacles
   once sat.

Motherland

after Tsvetaeva

Language is impossible
in a country like this. Even
the dictionary laughs when I look up
'England', 'Motherland', 'Home'.

It insists on falling open instead
three times out of the nine I try it
at the word Distance: 'Degree
of remoteness, interval of space.'

Distance: the word is ingrained like pain.
So much for England and so much
for my future to walk into the horizon
carrying distance in a broken suitcase.

The dictionary is the only one
who talks to me now. Says, laughing,
'Come back HOME!' but takes me
further and further away into the cold stars.

I am blue, bluer than water
I am nothing, for all I do
is pour syllables over aching brows.

England. It hurts my lips to shape
the word. This country makes me say
too many things I can't say. Home
of me, myself, my motherland.

A Letter to Dennis

in memoriam Dennis Potter

Deep in the strangest pits in England, deep
in the strangest forest, my grandfathers
and yours coughed out their silicotic lungs.
Silicosis. England. Land of phlegm,
and stereophonic gobbing, whose last pearls
of sputum on the lips, whose boils and tropes
and hallucinations are making me sick.

The point is how to find a use for fury,
as you have taught old father,
my old butt, wherever you are.
Still rude, I hope, still raucous and rejoicing
in the most painful erection in heaven
which rises through its carapace of sores
and cracking skin to sing in English.

You are as live to me as the tongue
in my mouth, as the complicated shame
of Englishness. Would you call me lass?
Would you heave up any stars for my crown?

Thetis

Thetis was a sea goddess who had the marvellous ability to change her shape. Peleus, a young man who had failed to win her over by persuasion, was taught by Proteus the way to overcome her: to bind her and hold on tightly whatever shape she took. The result of this forced union was Achilles.

No man can frighten me: watch as I stretch
my limbs for the transformation, I'm laughing
to feel the surge of other shapes beneath my skin.
It's like this: here comes the full thrill of my art
as the picture of a variegated
lizard insinuates itself into my mind.
I extend my neck, lengthen fingers, push
down toes to find the form. My back begins
to undulate, the skin to gleam. I think
my soul has slithered with me into this
shape as real as the little, long tongue in my mouth,
as the sun on my back, as the skill in absolute stillness.
My name is Thetis Creatrix and you,
voyeur, if you looked a little closer, would see
the next ripples spread up my bloody tail, to bloom
through this changing spine as the bark begins
to harden over my trunk. Already
I am so much the oak I lean everything towards
the black oxygen in the black air, I process
delicious gases through my personal chemistry,
suck moisture from the earth to a pulse so slow
you can't detect it. But my soul can read
the beat and is looking for a new language
to translate the pleasure of this power.
It's tigress. Low tremendous purrs start at the pit

of my stomach, I'm curving through long grass,
all sinew, in a body where tension
is the special joy and where the half-second
before a leap tells it all. Put out a paw
to dab a stone, an ant, a dead lamb. Life,
my life, is all play even up to the moment
when I'm tripped up, thrown down, bound, raped until
I bleed from my eyes, beaten out of shape,
forced to bring forth war.

Matthew Sweeney

Singing Class

There is this image of a tuning-fork
struck against a desk-top to loose
its lone note into a draughty room.
Then the vocal summits of the class

with one boy at least in their midst
dumb for an hour, mouthing air
the song-words flitting through his head
his eyes never leaving the inspector.

View from a Hammock

for Padraig Rooney

It is stained with wine, moored to a tree.
Around it the garden groups: roses, a table,
vines that have strayed too far north.

It hangs there, mostly unused.
Winds come, attempt to swirl it off –
it, made of holes tied together?

Help it, place your body there.
Feet head-high, arms loose –
climb there, sway on that absent sea.

Night is the best time: the dark
attentive to the skin. Midges are gone.
Spiders patrol the grass.

Hear the head empty of sounds.
Swing the eyes in an arc, on a city of
leaves, shutters, moonlit shreds of sky.

Captain Marsh

Captain Marsh has gone to work
in a locked room on the second floor.
He is not pleased by steps approaching.

We are close enough. Listen, he types
with two fingers and barks at mistakes
as if at insolent cabin-boys.

All winter he is marooned here
by his own orders. An electric fire
and a whisky-bottle are his comforts.

He has not spoken to us in months
though sometimes notes escape the room
requesting steak or lamb curry.

Nights when we can't sleep, we hear
the clacking of his machine far up
disturbing the pigeons on the rooftop.

What is his great vocation? When
will he reveal this late crop,
this surge that has replaced the sea?

We ask, make crude guesses, laugh.
Sometimes we wait outside the room
as he walks the boards as if in pain.

Imagined Arrival

White are the streets in this shabbiest-
grown of the world's great cities,
whiter than marshmallow angels.
Descending by parachute, one would be
arriving in a world long dead.
One would also be stiff with cold.

And if one, perhaps, would dangle there
in a skeletal tree, swigging brandy
from the equipment, rubbing fur ear-flaps,
one would have a view of the street
unhindered by involvement, as about one
the parachute would hang like snow.

And while getting one's wits back, groping
for a knife, a slow van would stop
leaving bottles of snow; and a man nearby
would dig the white from his steps
while a woman in a window opposite
might smile as he uncovered dirt.

By this stage pigeons would investigate
and one's toes would long be numb.
One would give up, and call for help
or if successful with the knife, drop down
leaving onlookers noticing the parachute
as one asked for soup and began to explain.

Preparation For Survival

for Philip Casey

Somewhere a man is swathed in furs
and is growing a beard of ice.
A survivor from an expedition
to set a flag at the absolute north
he chose to stay there
and learned to withstand cold.

He flies an aerial from the flagpole
and each month a plane leaves Greenland:
meat and coffee parachute down.
A temporary pleasure. The trade-
winds practise with pollen
above the submarines far south.

Audience at the war theatre,
fire will briefly light his sky
then a finite crackle on the radio.
Expert now in the disciplines of snow
he is learning to spear moose
or to fish through portholes in the ice.

The Applicants

They were turned away with a shake of hands,
a shrug, a live butt landing on the street.
Away they went through the maze of Soho,
avoiding bananas fallen from barrows, or
the diabolical eyes of men in doorways.
A clock chimed but they forgot to count.

He suggested a cappuccino, she agreed.
Ducking, he held the door open for her,
they sat beneath an angled, concave mirror.
Her circling spoon made the most noise
as he stared at a puddle on the formica.
That clock chimed again before they left.

They made a bleak picture at the busstop,
huddled there, in an imaginary rain.
The bus slowed, she was first to board –
a pixy figure, all of four feet tall,
and, as the queue advanced with smiles,
he followed, crouched to miss the ceiling.

Watches

He lifts a watch to his ear and listens,
all the time eyeing the Cherokee woman
stood alone at the bar with her gin
giving her own watch interrogations.
The barman behind her likes to whistle
Twenties tunes, and has ten hands.
She has two, and like a miniature star
that dropped on the street to roll in
through the legs of the drinkers, up
her long thigh, over the purple cotton
to rest on her wrist, the watch glints –
must be echt silver or something,
and there she's glancing at it again
so he listens to his to help time go,
arching his brows at those cheekbones
and the blackest hair he has ever seen.

Relics

The cleaver, hung on the scullery wall
these twenty years, gleamed once,
suffered the rasp of the backyard stone
to joint with ease the lambs he bought
on those monthly trips to Carn fair.
The basin that once caught lamb's blood
for black pudding, holds clothespegs
in the back bedroom where he slept
and on whose walls a holster hung
through my childhood, empty of its gun.
The backyard dancehall that he built
is a giant junkroom, with old papers
and coats, beds, prams, cans of paint.
The big house with poky rooms is flaking.
The mangle in the washhouse rolls
as it did for him, though the clothes
are machine-washed and spun dry.
The garden is a hedged-in field
where windfalls hide in the long grass.
The turkey stuffing alone survives
from his kitchen ways. The turfhouse walls
are rusted and patched with zinc,
and contain the hulk of the generator
by which, in advance of the government,
he brought electricity to the house.

Ends

At my end of the earth the Atlantic began.
On good days trawlers were flecks far out,
at night the green waves were luminous.
Gulls were the birds that gobbled my crusts
and the air in my bedroom was salty.
For two weeks once a whale decayed
on the pale beach while no one swam.
It was gelignite that cleared the air.

The uses of village carpenters were many.
Mine made me a pine box with a door,
tarpaulin-roofed, a front of fine-meshed wire.
It suited my friend, the albino mouse
who came from Derry and ate newspaper
and laid black grains on the floor.
When he walked his tail slithered behind.
And when I holidayed once, he starved.

The Boys in the Backroom

lean on a wall and talk about gold –
a blinding, twelve inch golden disc.
When they have it they will smash it
or melt it down to a yellow ball
to heave at a politician's window.

They will go on tour to Germany
and play a gig at the Reichstag
to a crowd as big as Hitler drew.
Airmen in wool-backed leather,
they will play through till dawn,

amps throwing their chords
across the lake to the iron East,
their words about epidemics,
freeze-outs, global shutdown,
fighting the hum of patrol boats.

They will buy out a Highland laird . . .
But their beer-break is over,
they flick their guitars alive,
take off behind the disused bar
and set the bare lightbulb dancing.

Cuba Street

Midnight on the Isle of Dogs.
Taxis gather on Cuba Street
like roaches in a kitchen.
Black stockings, foxes round the neck
and grey stilettos . . . They peer
through sodium fog at Rik's place.
Each has a passport of wine.
The throbs of a bass guitar
pass through them to the tankers
whose oil tints the water.
Purple bulbs down the stairs,
a woman's arm through the banisters
while a new friend fucks her . . .
Someone yells from the bathroom
for a corkscrew, and they
continue their hunt for Rik.
They unearth him in the bedroom
holding court by his coffin,
the black one on four legs.
He is explaining relativity
with patience to an art-
college crowd, his centre parting
impeccable as a fish skeleton,
his red line of a tie unstained.
He yawns, climbs in his coffin
onto stitched red satin
and stretches his white toes.
'Would you be a doll,' he whispers
to a girl in a tubular dress,
'and screw the lid down.
And muffle that awful band.'

The Submerged Door

The bridge by the chocolate shop
arcs like a rainbow whose hues
have drained to a pool of oil
motionless on the black water,
and a boy with a bicycle
dismounts here daily, climbs down
to the canal edge and kneels
peering into the water, moving
his gaze like a torch-beam
until it lights on the door,
and sometimes he reaches
through the oily wet to touch it,
sliding his fingers over panels
smooth from eels and water,
pausing at the letterbox,
and he imagines again the dawn-
crowd leaving the party,
taking the door with them,
laughing as it fell from the bridge,
floated, then slowly sank.

The Bats

The bats live in the old television aerials.
I hear them above me at night, and sometimes
one will blunder through the broken window,
glancing off me or the bulb, his sonar gone.

Since the hot weather, the parks are clay.
It's good to be up here, on the 13th floor
as the wind dips no lower, and when it rains
the two basins I leave on the roof get filled.

I'm clean, I drink, and I've a net for birds.
The lift broke last year so I don't get down
to the street much, and I don't have strength
to fight the market crowds for State rations.

From here I see the city, and the hills beyond
where I went often when the buses ran
though I try not to think of the dead years,
dead from the day they took the telephone.

If I could vote now I'd head the queue
but it's as likely as hearing a bat speak.
A million X's would have stopped their march
but who can loudly say he saw it coming?

I open the door to no one, I make no sound.
Ignore them: they may leave you alone.
I still have my books that I saved to read
and the bulb still comes on from ten to twelve.

Up on the roof at midday I sit in the shade
of a chimney, and I drink the breeze
while the bats hang from the aerials, immune
to the heat, to the unnatural height, to me.

I think, then, of the bats as companions.
There is one I watch more than the rest –
already I cross the roof to touch his head,
when he moves in his sleep I back away.

Down below I stay close to the window
and pluck my wrens in the afternoon
then hang them from the ex-telephone wire
while I snitch my four hours of sleep.

The Cold

After the all-hours drinking bout,
and the punchless acrimony,
he set off for the sea, on foot,
a good mile in the wind,
past zigzag lines of parked cars
and the disco din, past streetlights,
though if he'd needed light
the stars would have done –
down to the beach he wobbled,
a beercan in both pockets,
to sit on a rock and drink,
and think of his marriage,
and when both cans were empty
he removed his shoes
to walk unsteadily into the sea
and make for Iceland,
but the Atlantic sent him home again,
not a corpse, not a ghost,
to waken his wife
and complain of the cold.

Where Fishermen Can't Swim

Back there where fishermen can't swim,
where the ice-age coast of Donegal
leaves rocks among the waves,
a lobster-boat cast off, whose engine
croaked before the rocks were by.
The youngest in the crew leapt out
onto a rock to push the boat away,
then laughed when he couldn't jump back.
But exactly when did he realize
that the boat would float no nearer;
that all those pulls on the engine cord
would yield no shudders; that no rope
or lifebelt existed to be thrown;
that those flares were lost in cloud;
that the radio would bring a copter
an hour later? He had forty minutes –
to cling while the waves attacked,
to feel the rock gradually submerge.
And they had forty minutes of watching,
shouting into the radio, till he cried
out, sank from view, and stayed there.

The Lighthouse Keeper's Son

got arrested
as he wobbled home
on a lightless bicycle
after a late drink,
and he asked the cop
if the pockmarked moon
wasn't light enough
not to mention the Plough's
seven stars,
and his dad's beam
igniting the road
twice a minute,
then searching the sea
the umpteenth time
for nothing

A Couple Waiting

Leaving the door of the whitewashed house ajar
the man runs to the top of the hill
where he shields his eyes from the evening sun
and scans the sea. Behind him, a woman
holds a curtain back, but when he turns
and shakes his head, she lets the curtain fall.
She goes to the mirror beneath the flag
where she searches her face for signs of
the change her body tells her has begun.
The man shuts the door and sits at the table
where a chicken's bones are spread on two plates.
He thinks of his friends on the Atlantic,
coming up the western coast, laden
with well-wrapped bundles for his stable
that no horse uses. He thinks of his country,
and how his friends and he, with the help
of those bundles, would begin to set it right.
He calls the woman over and feels her stomach,
then asks why she thinks the boat is late.
Like him, she's harassed by an image –
the boat, searchlit, in French or Spanish waters,
guns pointed, a mouth at a megaphone.
Like him, she does not voice her mind,
instead sends him to the hill once more
in the dying light, to watch the red sun
sink in the water that's otherwise bare,
while she sits in the dark room, thinking
of the country their child will grow up in.

The Shadow Home

As his daughter watches from the doorway
she can't realize how exactly
she has got him right – how each time
he carries his kitbag to the bus
he will end his journey at another house
where another daughter will wait for him.
And another wife will embrace him,
as her mother did just now,
and all three will go inside.
What she doesn't know, his daughter, is where –
some corner of Connecticut,
some Atlantic island – there are no leads,
and she would never ask.
And does her shadow-sister look like her?
Is she blonde, is her mother blonde,
do they speak English, has her father
hidden a language for years?
And does he take his other daughter
on long walks through the pines,
and tell her about his travels,
about the people he's met, about himself?
There is so much about her father
she does not know, and so little time
between his absences to learn it.
Does her shadow-sister know about her,
or does she begin to suspect?
Which of the two is the shadow home?

On my Own

I stop, in my tracksuit, on a sleeper.
I lay my ear to the line
and if I hear a hum, slide
down the embankment, and wait
among the Coke-cans and beetles
till the express shakes by.
I think of last week, and McArdle
headless when the train had gone.
I scramble up to the tracks
that are blankly silver, and the sea
comes in view, and the young forest,
and the cross-country race I abandoned,
and my school's water tower – and I
head towards Dublin on my own.

The U-boat

I am floating by the wrecked U-boat,
naked as a dolphin in the August sun.
I've got away, again, from everyone.
I've moored my raft to the periscope
that stays underwater. On it I keep
my shorts and shoes, and Coca-Cola,
and a Bavarian girly magazine.
I've become so at-home in the ocean
that I think I must someday drown.
Miles away, on the edge of my hometown,
twin cooling towers fork the sky
where an airship phuts, selling beer.
No one knows the U-boat is here –
no boats approach these rocks,
no swimmers advance. I don't advertise.
I dive to the conning-tower and enter.
Bubbles speed behind me, above me,
but I am fast. I slide past my friend
the skeleton, until my breath runs low,
then I hit the surface he saw long ago
but never quite saw in the end.

A Postcard of a Hanging

for Padraig Rooney

I sent you a postcard of a hanging,
the first one I attended, not thinking
I'd like it, or even stand it, as you
must have loathed my postcard too
till you realized it must be a trick,
a decadent, oriental gimmick
to put liberals off their breakfast
of an egg, toast, jam and the rest.

I imagine your laughs then, the card
propped against the milk, as you read
again how I thrived in the East –
every meal a ginger and chilli feast;
the girls; the boys . . . how vibrant
the hours and how little I spent.
And you believed it, you knew
that all my varied antics were true.

And you turned to the picture again,
a colour print – a gallows, two men,
one hooded, one holding a noose
of whitest rope, for the moment loose,
and low in the foreground, a crowd
of men mainly, silently loud,
all Eastern, except for two or three –
one of whom, if you look closely, is me.

Symmetry

Gentlemen, you will please wear a tie
while peeing. And in the criss-cross corridors
you will pass without touching,
as you journey to and from the dining-room
under the portraits of Prime Ministers,
(except for the woman). You will sit
equally spaced apart, four facing four,
with one (each of you in turn) facing me
down the long, driftwood table.
While eating, you needn't call me Sir.

Two legs of lamb must be carved
simultaneously. Decide among yourselves.
And eat as much or as little as you like
but eat the same. Your weights
must match at the end as at the start;
must be half of mine. And no glass
can go empty of blood-red wine
till the clock-hands cross at midnight
when I will retire. Leaving nine.
Gentlemen, you will please set that right.

Pink Milk

When the goats ate the red carnations
and the next morning's milk was pink,
the abbot loved it, demanded more

but the monks loved their flower-garden
and turned to cochineal, to crushed ants,
to paprika, all stirred in milk

to no avail – the perfume was gone
and the abbot grumpy, so carnations
were sacrificed to rampant goats

whose beards jigged as they chewed,
who looked up at the watching monks
while the abbot watched from a window

and in the kitchen, a leg of pork
thawed on a hook from the ceiling,
and blood dripped into a milk-jug.

Tube Ride to Martha's

Before the sirens started, he was late –
late for a dinner at his woman's,
but he'd managed to find a good Rioja
and an excellent excuse: his cat
had burned her tail in the toaster
(this was true) and he'd brought her
to the vet and back in a cab.
He thought about a third cab to Martha's
but funds were low, and the tube ride
was four stops, a half hour with the walks.
He had a thriller in his carrier-bag,
a Ross McDonald, long out of print,
which he opened on the escalator, wanting
it finished tonight. When the smoke came
he hardly noticed, till the black guard
tried to hustle everyone upstairs,
and trains rushed by, without stopping,
and people pushed and screamed.
As the smoke got thicker and blacker
with flames growing fast, he realized
it was over, almost before it had begun.

Blue Shoes

I see that day's non-headlines, as he did
        though they're smoky now –
a prince at playschool, a brat's betrothal.
Some days they rob the gossip entries
        in lieu of disasters.
        They missed his later.

The weather inch reads more like Sicily
        than England. I see him
hurrying towards the train, his hand
raised to his eyes, the sunglasses at home.
        I have his notes here,
        the last of any consequence.

All the women, it seems, wore blue shoes
        in keeping with the morning.
He played with patterns, with omens
he deciphered later. That particular day
        it was blue shoes
        for want of any better.

I see him with a letter and xeroxed map
        leaving the station.
He is sucking mints, perhaps hungover.
At the school gates he checks his flies.
        He goes in the office,
        is lost from sight.

Did they know the strain of these visits?
        Did the kids care?
It was a long day, but not outlandish.
In his honour they had lunch in a pub.
        On another day
        it would have relaxed him.

He was chauffeured to the train in the end,
    an overwound watch.
He queued at a phone, his heart chugging.
A woman was speaking, a man waiting –
    the woman, he wrote,
    wore blue shoes.

Hard for me in this library to imagine
    that home journey,
the mounting pain in his mind and chest,
the prison of that train in motion.
    All I know is
    he thought he was dead.

And got off at a suburban station
    to ride in an ambulance
through all the jams of South London
to nurses and a narrow bed with wheels
    and electric wires
    on feet, wrists and heart.

I am reading over his own description
    of that evening –
how later, at home, he imagined
he'd got away with it, and drank.
    He got away
    for the time being.

For years, even, but what does it matter –
    he never forgot
that day of the interrupted train,
the only time in his life, late sun
    and pretty women
    wearing blue shoes.

Gold

The gold bars lie buried in the silt
and three skeletons lie guarding them,
three males, though the squid who sleeps
in the first skull couldn't say
and couldn't care less. To her
it is a cave, a domed cavern
she shares with no one. And who
could expect her to guess the plans
that had pulsed there, stalled,
till the ship reached Spain – expect her
to dream the face of the new wife
whose image had lodged there,
the image that faded with death?
The second skull lies yards away
from its long bones, and this one
is empty. But this one, too,
had taken in Spanish and spoken it out,
and had often eyed the gold.
Its eye-holes stare there still.
A crab sits in the third skull,
watching – a spider gone hard.
He is dictator of this stretch
of water, and the fact that he sits
in the skull of a Captain
is as useless to him as gold.
And nowhere on the skull wall
is a wisp of the knowledge
that the Captain's villa is ruined.
And the gold bars were going there
unknown to the crew. And unknown
to the divers whose boat churns above –
all they know is there's gold here.

Me and Benjy

Me and Benjy, my teddybear,
went to bed to sleep.
What else would we do but sleep?
We couldn't, however –
the noise was atrocious,
shouting and laughing,
thumping and whooping –
Just imagine if that was us,
I whispered in Benjy's ear,
Guzzling wine and beer,
making one hell of a fuss!
What are we going to do?
I looked into Benjy's eyes,
Benjy's brownglass eyes.
Benjy, it has to be you,
I said, throwing him out,
then sliding out myself,
knocking a book from a shelf
with a thump, and a shout
from downstairs: *Go to sleep!*
The cheek of it, I thought.
One of their party ought
to investigate sleep-
possibilities up here,
to lie down on our bed,
pull the pillow over her head,
and ignore down there!
Come on Benjy, let's go.
We crept down the stairs,
me and that Benjybear,
and walked on tiptoe

to the living-room din
that vibrated the floor.
I pulled open the door
and chucked Benjy in.

The Aunt I Never Met

The aunt I never met was black-haired
and holy. She sang in the choir
on Sundays. She also helped
my grandfather butcher the lambs
he kept in the long grass at the back –
even he agreed she was the best
with the cleaver. She played tennis
with priests, and beat them,
and drank Bloody Marys from a bottle
during whist drives, and owned
the only yellow bubblecar in Ulster
(now in a private collection
in Guernsey). During the war
she took up German, crossed her sevens,
lit the odd bonfire at night
on the cliff edge, and did no good.
French toast and salmon were her favourites.
She hated kids – her eventual undoing,
if you ask me. Why else did she
end her days in that old farmhouse
hidden by trees, where the outside light
stayed on all night to lure
visitors, even family, who never came?
Why else did I never meet her?

Biscuit Men

Making biscuits shaped like men,
baking them until they're brown,
eating all the heads, and then . . .
He always got stuck here, as though
he was one of the biscuit men,
and the cardboard woman he imagined
singing the nursery rhyme
in the piny kitchen   was standing
by his elbow in the study
where he went every day to try
to get past these rhymes,
to bleed them out of his head.

But they wouldn't go, and she
was down on the street again,
beneath his window, bags at her feet,
while a cabbie braked,
then reached up to switch off
his yellow light, as she got in
without a glance up at him
where he'd stand for hours.
. . . dumping them into the bin . . .
Dumping one . . . He still had a head
that was full of nursery rhymes
or bits, and she was their star.

Cacti

After she left he bought another cactus
just like the one she'd bought him
in the airport in Marrakesh. He had to hunt
through London, and then, in Camden,
among hordes of hand-holding kids
who clog the market, he found it,
bought it, and brought it home to hers.
Next week he was back for another,
then another. He was coaxed into trying
different breeds, bright ones flashing red –
like the smile of the shop-girl
he hadn't noticed. He bought a rug, too,
sand-coloured, for the living room,
and spent a weekend repainting
the walls beige, the ceiling pale blue.
He had the worn, black suite re-upholstered
in tan, and took to lying on the sofa
in a brown djellaba, with the cacti all around,
and Arab music on. If she should come back,
he thought, she might feel at home.

Hanging

Hanging from the lamppost
he could see far –
cars parked to the street's end,
the few late-night walkers
most of whom ignored him
hanging there. He could hear
screams and running feet,
also quick shuffles away
and, eventually, the wah-wahs
that came with blue lights
that led in the dawn.
Then the lights in all the houses
went on, and dressing-gown
wearers gathered, killing yawns.
And flashbulbs exploded,
though he couldn't hold
his head up, and his face
was blue. A megaphone
asked the crowd to go home
as a ladder leant on the lamppost
for someone to ascend.
He looked into this man's eye
as the knife cut him down.

Surplus Light

Could be the making of your marriage,
or of your divorce. Try it at dusk,
when it comes into its own. Sit there
at my window with the curtains open,
as daylight shrinks behind silhouettes
of buildings like my own. See how
its headstart leaves the others standing
(which, of course, they are), even though
one hour later they're a staggered line
of lit streetlights on a night street.

Hard for you, I expect, to imagine
the effect on the nerves of witnessing
such relentless light, of seeing it
take on the sun and wear it down.
That's apart from its unlikely beauty –
my *iron star-tree* I could call it
but I won't. And to think that I rang
the Council to complain! What are rates
compared to this gift of surplus light,
this permanent reminder of wastage?

The Desert

He wanted *rim-bel-terfass* and nothing else.
He wanted a space-shot of the desert.
He wanted that Algerian woman he'd known
years before, who'd fed him *couscous*,
with rosewater made by her own mother.
He'd had a male friend who taught there,
on an oasis — he wanted him back there,
arriving, in the small hours, once a year
with dates, and goat-cheese, and the strong
red wines that held their own in France.
He wanted to be able to visit him —
take the train from Algiers, a rucksack
with bacon and whiskey on his back,
no advance warning, no Arabic, no French —
and send a series of postcards to himself
till, one by one, they all arrived back.

rim-bel-terfass: a stew made of gazelle meat, with Saharan truffles
(Sahara dish). *Larousse Gastronomique*

Artificial Blood

As the artificial blood that saved him
was Japanese, he went to live in Japan.
And of course he found the raw fish
the best for his patched-up heart.
The doctors were reassuring too,
even if they spoke a stretched English
and couldn't laugh. He kept in touch
with his golfer son – golf was played
throughout Japan; perhaps one day
his son would visit with saké . . .
Some nights he'd walk to a noodle bar
and point, then eat. He'd hurry
past the geisha parlours, and maybe
he'd stop at a phone, then stay outside
till he was too tired to remember
those walks on the Malvern Hills
he'd taken too seldom, too long ago
when his son was little, his wife alive,
before his heart operation,
before the white, thin artificial blood
entered his body and led him to Japan.

New Rules

Even his dog ran with a limp,
following his lopsided run
along the path by the River Wye
where cyclists came up behind,
ringing their tinny bells, shouting
when the dog wouldn't limp aside,
and the man wouldn't either.

And you had to agree with them,
the lame dog and the lame man.
Even to get into a tracksuit lame
is admirable. But to go running,
or what passed for it, and to buy
a lame dog, or lame a good dog –
that's when you're talking new rules.

The Blind Men

They want it back, the blind men,
students of magnified touch,
evictees from this dingy house
whose bare walls they know by heart.
They want back in, and me out.
They still have keys they use
at night, to let me know –
by black hairs in the bath,
by a white stick under the stairs,
by tapping on bedroom doors
then not being there – that they
are the rightful tenants here,
and I've got to go. So I keep
the radio on, no television.
I stand in the mirrorless bathroom
and shave by touch, shivering
from the linoless floor. I cook
in the half-dark, and rarely work.
I keep my books hidden.
It's not as if it's a mansion –
the basement flooded last year,
as they will know, and the attic-
ladder's kaput – it's nowhere
to throw a party in, even if
people could find the street,
but they want it back, the blind men,
and they're not getting me out.

Asleep in a Chair

Asleep in a chair for three hours?
Take that man away. Bind him
and bundle him into a mini-cab,
drive through the Southern English night
till you see the lights of Brighton,
then throw him out on the South Downs.

Hopefully it will be sub zero
and wet as Ireland. (*Drunk* and
asleep in a chair for three hours,
with the TV and the gas fire on?)
Pick a field with cattle in it,
or better still, a nervy horse.

Make sure there's no stream near,
or even a house. Get miles away
from a shop or a chemist –
empty out his pockets just in case.
Smash his glasses while you're at it.
Forget you liked him, lose his name.

Burn his shoes to ash beside him,
keep his jeans as a souvenir.
Cut his hair off (*all* his hair).
Asleep in a chair for three hours?
By the time you're finished, honey,
he might have learned to sleep in a bed.

Monkey

Even when the monkey died
they never invited us round
to eat green banana curry
and play braille scrabble
in that room underground
where twin hammocks hung
near the dead monkey's cage
that held him still, stuffed
and gutted, body-shampooed,
face locked in a rage
that quick death provides.
And none of us knew
what went on at the end,
whether poison, or heart,
or if one of them blew
their monkey away,
then turned on the other
and aimed that Luger,
that well-oiled Luger
at the brain of a brother,
but flung the gun down.
And with their excuse gone
we expected invites,
one big wake, perhaps,
complete with champagne,
and Joe, the taxidermist,
waiving his bill –
his grief-contribution,
his goody for the party.
We're all waiting still.

After Closing Time

Those who don't believe in life after death should be here after closing time. [Notice inside an office in Derry's city cemetery]

The gate will be open, and streetlights
will guide you through the graves,
but you'd better watch your carry-outs
as the dead are barred from pubs.
Watch for the flowers that fly
from grave to grave, creating letters
for the papers and maybe more dead –
and one thing you'll know in the half-light
is that the dead are too many
to fit in the ground, too lively
to lie in a box, so they do
what you'd expect them to, and that's why
they surround you as you swig
from a can. They ruffle your hair,
breathe through unbrushed teeth,
fart even, and one of the pushier
puts his finger in the hole in his head
then invites you to follow. Another
opens his rotting shirt to show you
his two hearts, the old and the new,
and a one-legged ex-pensioner
eyes the bulge of your cigarettes,
and you'd be well advised to drain
one can, then chuck the other
as far as you're able, for the dead
hate those who outlive them,
and you'd be canny to suss this
and run, and hope the gate's not shut.

Donegal, Arizona

for Dermot Seymour

He put Donegal in the oven,
cooked it awhile, and got Arizona.
And he siphoned all that rain
and the troublesome Atlantic
into waterholes in the desert
and the Colorado River.
A few tons of gelignite
moved the hills together
to make the Grand Canyon,
and he stretched all the toads
to make Gila monsters,
and bought a few steamboats,
and buried gold in the hills.
The Indians were difficult
but he advertised abroad,
then the Mexican ambassador
signed the Treaty of Guadalupe
all over again, and Derry
stared at Sligo over a void.

Flat Bird

Forced off the pavement
by my own hurry
and three women walking abreast,
I spy a blob on the tarmac
like a map of a country
or a pattern in cement,
and as I step over it
I really look at it,
till I see what it is –
I don't want to believe it
but it's a flat bird,
a totally flat bird.

It's hard to make out
what kind of bird.
It's hard to imagine it airborne,
or having a third dimension,
or ever being heard.
Did that driver shout,
who crushed the skull,
and left the bird dead
for other drivers to flatten?
How long did it take to happen,
to make a flat bird,
a totally flat bird?

The Bells

for John Hartley Williams

Fighting the undertow,
watching the boat drift away,
the monk felt his habit grow
heavy as a suit of armour,
and struggled till he was naked,
hoping his fat would keep him
alive in the ice-berged Atlantic
until he caught the toe of rock
that kicked the sea to Ireland.
He clung to a plastic lunchbox
and thought of the veal pies
famous in the monastery, hoping
his surfeit years were enough
to keep him awake for five hours.
He thought of his antics
with the boy, behind the shed
where his boat was kept
waiting for today. He felt
his fingers get pins and needles
and his testicles go numb,
his feet become bare bone
and his eyes start to close.
He was so tired now,
already he heard the bells ring
in the distant fog. If he slept
he'd float there, in time for mass.

The Bridal Suite

for Nuala hí Dhomhnaill

On the third night in the bridal suite
without the bride, he panicked.
He couldn't handle another dream like that,
not wet, like he'd expected,
but not dry either – men digging holes
that they'd fill with water, donkeys
crossing valleys that suddenly flooded.
The alarm-call had a job to wake him,
to send him out from the huge bed,
past the corner kissing-sofa, up two steps
to the shower he hardly needed,
where he'd scrub himself clean as the baby
he'd hoped to start that night,
under the canopy like a wimple,
in that room of pinks and greens.
Naked and dripping, he'd rung Reception
to see if she'd rung, then he'd stood
looking out at the new marina,
as if he'd glimpse her on a yacht.
On the third night he could take no more –
he dressed, to the smell of her perfume,
and leaving her clothes there,
the wedding dress in a pile in the wardrobe,
he walked past the deaf night porter,
out to his car. He had no idea
where he was headed, only that she,
if she ever came back, could sample
the bridal suite on her own,
could toss in that canopied bed
and tell him about her dreams.

The Blue Taps

He left me the blue taps
from his blue bath.
He left me the cacti he spoke to.
I had to go and take them
from his grey house
before she sold it.
I had to stand there
in the blue living room
and ask her the names
he'd given all the cacti.
I had to leave her
with no taps in the bathroom.
She didn't seem to care.
I wanted to ask her
why he'd been blue-crazy,
or was she in it, too?
I wanted to know
how long they'd taken
to gather fifteen cacti,
and why he'd spoken to them.
I asked none of this,
just ferried my heirlooms
to the back seat of my car.
I hoped the taps fitted.
I hoped I could remember
the cacti's names
in the correct order.
I had a white bath,
but my living room was green.

The Compromise

He wanted to be buried on the moon.
At last he was answering the question
but she wouldn't have it. She laughed
and he laughed, but he persisted.
He brought it up at dinner parties.
He wrapped it in a joke, but she
knew he meant it. A guest said
there wouldn't be many at the funeral.
No maggots, though, another said,
and no graffiti on the gravestone,
at least for a decade or three.
She brought up the cost. He shrugged,
spoke of sponsorship, of ice-
preservation, of the enabling future.
He would be famous dead. A guest
proposed a grave on Iona, among
the graves of kings. Mentioned
that only twice had men landed
on the moon, and they were living.
Suggested writing to one. And asking
about grave-sites, she added.
He was undeflected. He repeated
he wanted to be buried on the moon,
whatever it took. He went quiet.
A fifth cork was popped, then he
offered a compromise, a heart-coffin
snug in the hold of a space-shuttle,
his heart in there, the rest of him
in Highgate, in Derry, in the sea.
They were all delighted to agree.

An End

I want to end up on Inishtrahull,
in the small graveyard there
on the high side of the island,
carried there in a helicopter sling
with twenty speedboats following.
And I want my favourite Thai chef
flown there, a day before,
and brought to the local fishermen
so he can serve a chilli feast
before we head off up the hill.
A bar, too, it goes without saying,
free to all, the beer icy,
the whiskey Irish, and loud
through speakers high on poles
the gruff voice of Tom Waits
causing the gulls to congregate.
Get Tom himself there, if you can.
And in the box with me I want
a hipflask filled with Black Bush,
a pen and a blank notebook,
all the vitamins in one bottle,
my address book and ten pound coins.
Also, a Cantonese primer.
I want no flowers, only cacti
and my headstone must be glass.

Acknowledgements

The poems in this selection are taken from the following books, to whose publishers acknowledgement is made: *Bestiary* (Bloodaxe, 1997), *Secrets* (Bodley Head, 1994), *Recovering a Body* (Bloodaxe, 1994) and *Short Days, Long Nights, New and Selected Poems* (Bloodaxe, 1991) for Helen Dunmore; *Electroplating the Baby* (Bloodaxe, 1988), *Phrase Book* (OUP, 1992) and *Motherland* (Gwaithel & Gilwern, 1996) for Jo Shapcott; *A Round House* (Allison & Busby, 1983), *The Lame Waltzer* (Allison & Busby, 1985), *Blue Shoes* (Secker & Warburg, 1989), *The Flying Spring Onion* (Faber & Faber, 1992), *Cacti* (Secker & Warburg, 1992), *Fatso in the Red Suit* (Faber & Faber, 1995) and *The Bridal Suite* (Jonathan Cape, 1997) for Matthew Sweeney.